PLANNING INSTRUCTION FOR ADULT LEARNERS

PLANNING INSTRUCTION
for Adult Learners

Patricia Cranton
Brock University

Wall & Emerson, Inc.
Toronto, Ontario • Middletown, Ohio

An earlier version of Chapter Five was first published in the *Journal of Higher Education,* Vol. 57, No. 3 (May/June 1986). Copyright 1986 Ohio State University Press. All rights reserved. Reprinted here with permission.

The author gratefully acknowledges the valuable assistance of Professor Cynthia B. Weston of McGill University, co-author of Chapters Two and Five of this book, and her kind permission to publish those chapters here.

The author gratefully acknowledges the permission of Professor Gerald M. Torkelson, Professor Emeritus, University of Washington, to reproduce his diagram of the Concept Cone, and of the Concrete-Abstract Continuum developed by Professor Torkelson and Dr. C. O. Bergeson, Emeritus Professor of Education, State University of New York—Albany

Requests for permission to make copies of any part of this work should be sent to: Wall & Emerson, Inc., Six O'Connor Drive, Toronto, Ontario, Canada M4K 2K1

Orders for this book may be directed to either of the following addresses:

For the United States:	*For Canada and the rest of the world:*
Wall & Emerson, Inc.	Wall & Emerson, Inc.
3210 South Main St.	Six O'Connor Drive
P. O. Box 448686	Toronto, Ontario, Canada
Middletown, Ohio 45044-8686	M4K 2K1

By telephone or facsimile (for both addresses):
Telephone: (416) 467-8685
Fax: (416) 696-2460

Canadian Cataloguing in Publication Data

Cranton, Patricia
  Planning instruction for adult learners

Includes bibliographical references and index.
ISBN 0-921332-24-6

1. Adult education. 2. Teaching. I. Title.

LC5219.C73 1989   374'.02   C89-093672-2

Printed in Canada by Webcom.
  2 3 4 5   95 94 93 92

TABLE OF CONTENTS

CHAPTER ONE
PRINCIPLES OF ADULT LEARNING

Adult educators are faced with the complex task of planning courses in their areas of expertise or interest, often with very little or no training in how to teach. A simple and common solution to this dilemma is to follow the format of an established textbook and to rely on familiar teaching methods, usually those we experienced as students. However, with different groups of learners in different instructional settings, this simple solution can lead to the frustrating feeling that the needs of the learner are not being met and there must be a better way to teach.

Venturing into the world of education courses or the literature on how to teach will offer some guidance, but will still leave the adult educator with the suspicion that there must be a better way to teach.

It is the intent of this book to integrate what we know about how adults learn with the principles of designing instruction. A practical procedure for the planning of any type of instruction for adults will be provided. A two-hour professional development workshop, a general interest session, a graduate course, or individualized tutoring can be planned using the same procedure, even though the actual instructional strategies may look completely different.

The process of planning instruction for adults is described in six steps in the following chapters.

In Chapter Two, *Considering the Audience*, the principles of adult learning are described, along with their implications for instruction. It is important to gather as much information as possible regarding the characteristics of the learners: age, work experience, educational experience, special needs, interests, reasons for involvement in the instruction. This chapter will review these characteristics, their implications for planning, and techniques for collecting relevant information.

One of the first steps in planning instruction is to select the topics to be included. This can also be described as considering what the learners will get out of the instruction: the goals or objectives. Chapter Three, *Objectives*, discusses the basics of writing objectives, the domains and levels of expected learning, and negotiating or co-operatively developing objectives with adult learners.

Chapter Four, *Sequencing Instruction*, presents guidelines for planning the order in which objectives will be met. In structured disciplines such as mathematics or sciences, it is quite clear that some topics must be mastered before others can be attempted; the content is hierarchical, and concepts depend on or incorporate others. In other areas, these dependencies may not be as clear, or may not exist at all. How does the instructor determine the sequence of instruction? How much input can the learner have into this process?

Chapter Five, *Developing the Instructional Strategy*, reviews the wide array of methods and materials available to the adult educator. The selection of appropriate instructional strategies may well be the most complex decision in planning instruction; the choices are dependent on the characteristics of the learner, the nature of the expected learning, the size of the group, the facilities available, the instructor's skills and preferences.

The planning, selecting, and developing of techniques to evaluate learner performance, either for feedback or for grading purposes, are addressed in Chapter Six, *Evaluating Learning*. Again, the selection of techniques should include consideration of the characteristics of the learner, the subject area, and the instructional setting.

Chapter Seven, *Evaluating the Instruction*, describes a procedure for assessing the quality of the instruction. Monitoring the effectiveness of the instruction is as much a part of teaching as is monitoring the amount and quality of participants' learning.

Background

At present, there are two distinct relevant areas in the literature of educational theory: the systematic design of instruction and adult education. This book has its foundations in both areas.

Instructional design is sometimes described as the "technology of education." The foundation of instructional design lies in behavioral psychology, with its basic idea that if learning is broken down into small, observable, sequential steps with immediate reinforcement provided, almost anyone can learn anything. When that concept is used in the planning of instruction, it yields a model which can be very useful. We need to know what is going to be learned, the sequence in which it is learned, the best methods for achieving that learning, and techniques for reinforcing the learning. Instructional design has provided procedures for the development of numerous individualized learning packages, modules, courses, and programs.

Many educators, though, object to systematic instructional design. It simply *sounds* too technical; it seems to take away the "art" of education; it seems too structured; it seems to deny creativity and flexibility in teaching. We all now know that behavioral psychology did not consider the individual cognitive processes and hence ignored the most important aspect of learning. Unfortunately, educators have the tendency to throw out the good with the bad. In recent years, educational research has demonstrated, if nothing else, that the teaching and learning process is an extremely complex interaction between individuals and the environment. Learners are *not* the same as Skinner's pigeons. But this does not necessarily imply that we need to throw out systematic planning of instruction. Research in the 1960s clearly demonstrated that individuals learn more effectively when they know what they are expected to learn (objectives), learn more effectively when they have the prerequisites to the learning (sequencing), and learn more effectively when they receive feedback (evaluation). The instructional design model remains a valuable and widely used procedure for planning.

As soon as we turn to the adult education literature, instructional design seems to be completely irrelevant. We are told that the adult learner is self-directed, knows what he or she wants to learn, and must have input into that learning. The instructor becomes a facilitator of the learning; instruction is really group interaction. The adult should judge his or her own learning, evaluate his or her own progress; this is no longer the role of the instructor.

Adult education literature will be difficult for most new instructors of adults to absorb or implement. The whole idea that an instructor is someone who stands in front of a class seems to be wrong.

Neither position is wrong; the two points of view do not have to be contradictory. It is essential that instruction be carefully planned, including consideration of the characteristics of the audience. It is also essential that adults be treated as adults, that they be respected for their backgrounds and experiences, that they be "allowed" to interact with each other, and that they not be threatened by the expert who has the power of grading them.

It is the position, throughout this book, that the principles of instructional design can be applied to the education of adults. Objectives can be developed for, with, or by adult learners. Sequencing can be determined for or with the agreement of the adult audience. The selection of instructional strategies must be based on the characteristics of the audience, as well as on the nature of the expected learning. Evaluation techniques are sometimes informal, sometimes formal, but evaluation of learning must always be a component of the teaching and learning process. And, every educator should assess the effectiveness of his or her own instruction.

It is difficult to address the requirements of every adult education situation simultaneously. The workshop leader for a professional development activity has quite different concerns from the instructor of a university-level course. The planning process may be the same, but the requirements of the setting or context in which the teaching and learning takes place will be quite different. The workshop leader will not be required to assign a grade and consequently will not be concerned about formal testing. The university instructor will have a greater chance to get to know his students and will not be as concerned about pre-assessment of audience characteristics. Nevertheless, each component of the instructional design model can be seen to exist in each situation.

Definitions

Instructional design is defined as the systematic planning of instruction, including considering the audience, setting objectives, sequencing instruction, selecting instructional strategies, evaluating learning, and evaluating instructional effectiveness. The instructional designer is the individual responsible for these activities, whether it be the instructor or the curriculum developer.

Adult education is defined as any organized, sustained activity engaged in by adult individuals for the purposes of changing their knowledge, skills, or values in any area.

A learner is any individual who engages in educational activities for the purposes of acquiring knowledge, skills, or values in any area. The term, student, is generally avoided since it connotes a younger learner, but when used, it is equivalent to learner.

An instructor is any individual who facilitates or directs learning. The role of an instructor may include expert, manager, teacher, evaluator, facilitator, leader, mentor, or instructional designer.

Theoretical Foundations

As an area of academic investigation, adult education is in its infancy. Although instruction has been offered to adult audiences in some form throughout history, training for adult educators at colleges or universities is relatively recent. Consequently, it is only in the last few decades that departments or programs of adult education have existed. With the development of courses, programs, and departments, educational researchers have turned to adult education as an area of study and have begun to describe theoretical models relevant to instruction for adult learners.

It should be stated, before we travel too far into this bewildering world, that a *theory* is simply an explanation of facts or observations and the relationships among those facts or observations. If an instructor was to observe, for example, that standing over and yelling at individuals in his group seemed to cause them to cringe, cover their ears, and eventually become quite anxious and fearful, he might develop a theory that loud noises increased anxiety. This theory could be tested further, other variables could be included to make sure that it really was the loud noise that caused the apprehension, and so on. But the theory is the explanation of the relationship between the two observed behaviors—yelling and cringing.

Theories are developed in two ways. Someone may have an idea or a "hunch" of how things are related, then collect information to prove or disprove that hunch. Or someone may collect data (observations), then from those data develop an explanation for them. Most theories are developed slowly and carefully over many years; even then, serious pitfalls can be encountered. We might observe, throughout a lifetime, that 99% of people eat dill pickles; we might also observe and collect extensive data to show that 99% of all individuals die. An obvious theory would be that eventually dill pickles kill people. However ridiculous this example of a theory may be, it is an easy enough mistake to make when observing the complex instruction and learning processes.

So why bother with theories? Theories provide us with a way of summarizing, explaining, and understanding the multitude of complex behaviors we may observe. For the practitioner, a theory provides guidelines for effective practice. If we know that behaviors are related in a certain way, it allows us to predict that if we act in a certain way, certain results will follow. Unfortunately, such clear-cut theory-based guidelines are not available for instructors. However, it remains invaluable for the practitioner of adult education to utilize and build upon the results of theoreticians and researchers.

A brief summary of the theoretical foundations of adult education will be provided. It is not the purpose of this book to describe in detail or to analyze the work done in this area; the interested reader is referred to the books and articles listed in the bibliography for further study.

Theories of Instruction

No unified theory of instruction for adult learners exists. It can also be argued that no *one* theory of instruction is possible, given the diverse activities that are, together, called adult education.

However, several theoretical writers have provided the foundations for adult education practice, even though they may not have been writing directly about adult education.

Many of the current approaches and thoughts in adult education can be traced directly to the writings of Dewey (1916, 1938). Lindeman (1926) extended Dewey's work in order to provide one of the earliest descriptions of adult education. Dewey argued that education must be thought of as a lifelong process, rather than the shaping of young minds. He viewed learning as being based on life experience, and emphasized the importance of the scientific method in learning. That is, an individual faced with a problem will develop hypotheses about the problem and then collect evidence to confirm or deny these hypotheses. These ways of describing learning lead to a model of instruction in which the teacher's role is one of guide and facilitator rather than expert or formal authority. A teacher's activities would include:

1. The selection of experiences for and with the learner;

2. The consideration of the learner's needs and past experiences;

3. Participation in co-operative or mutual learning experiences; and

4. Utilizing the environment in learning experiences.

Freire's (1973) work can be thought of as critical theory rather than theory: he describes how things should or could be rather than describing how things *are*, as a true theorist does. Freire worked in Brazil in the area of literacy education. He believes that lack of education, particularly literacy education, is a form of oppression. The role of the educator is to understand and become a part of the learner's culture, to stimulate learning, and hence to "free" or empower the individual. This thinking may seem radical, but several implications for North American adult education can be drawn from Freire's writings:

1. The educator becomes a learner, listening to and understanding the needs of the individual;

2. Learners participate actively in the learning process, through dialogue with the instructor (co-learner); and

3. Educator and learner are mutually responsible for the teaching and learning process.

The strongest influence on the practice of adult education has been the writings of Malcolm Knowles (1978, 1980, 1984). Although the term "andragogy" was used prior to Knowles' work, he is credited with popularizing the term, which is defined as the "art and science of helping adults learn" (Knowles 1980, 30). Knowles later wrote that "andragogy is simply another model of assumptions about learners to be used alongside the pedagogical model of assumptions" (Knowles 1980, 43). However, Knowles' theory (or model) of instruction for adult learners has guided practitioners and researchers in adult education for the last 15 years.

Knowles' approach rests on four basic assumptions about the "art and science of helping adults learn."

1. It is a normal aspect of the process of maturation for a person to move from dependency toward increasing self-directedness, but at different rates for different people and in different stages of life.

Teachers have a responsibility to encourage and nurture this movement towards independence. Adults have a deep psychological need to be generally self-directing, although they may be dependent in particular temporary situations.

2. As people grow and develop, they accumulate an increasing reservoir of experience that becomes an increasingly rich resource for learning—for themselves and for others. Furthermore, people attach more meaning to learnings they gain from experience than to those they acquire passively. Accordingly, the primary techniques in education are experiential techniques—laboratory experiments, discussion, problem-solving cases, simulation exercises, field experience, and the like.

3. People become ready to learn something when they experience a need to learn it in order to cope more effectively with real-life tasks or problems. The educator has a responsibility to create conditions and provide tools and procedures for helping learners discover their "need to know." And learning programs should be organized around life-application categories and sequenced according to the learners' readiness to learn.

4. Learners see education as the process of developing increased competence to achieve their full potential in life. They want to be able to apply whatever knowledge and skill they gain today to living more effectively tomorrow. Accordingly, learning experiences should be organized around competency-development categories. People are performance-centered in their orientation to learning.

Based on these assumptions, Knowles and other writers have provided detailed implications for practice and suggestions for research and theory-building. Some implications of Knowles' theory have become commonly accepted practice in adult education.

1. The learning climate, both physical and psychological, should be carefully constructed. The physical environment should be one in which adults feel at ease—informally arranged and decorated, with sufficient light and good acoustics. The psychological environment should be one of acceptance, respect, and support, where freedom of expression exists, without fear of punishment or ridicule.

2. The adult's desire for self-direction is in direct conflict with the traditional practice of instructor-directed learning. The implication here is that learning needs should be diagnosed by the learner: The instructor should construct a model of the competencies or characteristics required to achieve a given ideal model of performance; provide diagnostic experiences in which the learners can assess their present level of competencies in the light of those portrayed in the model; and help the learners to measure the gaps between their present competencies and those required by the model (Knowles 1980, 47–48).

3. Learners should be involved in the process of planning their own learning, with the instructor acting as a guide and resource person.

4. The teaching and learning process is the *mutual* responsibility of the instructor and the learner. The instructor's role is one of resource person, co-inquirer, facilitator, catalyst, guide.

5. "Nothing makes an adult feel more childlike than being judged by another adult; it is the ultimate sign of disrespect and dependency, as the one who is being judged experiences it" (Knowles 1980, 49). Following the andragogical assumptions, the adult learner would be involved in self-evaluation, with the instructor assisting the learners in obtaining evidence for themselves about the progress they are making toward their goals. Knowles describes evaluation in terms of re-diagnosis of learning needs.

6. Adults are a rich resource of experience; the instructional techniques should utilize this resource. Therefore, emphasis can be placed on discussions, problem-solving exercises, group work, case studies, role-playing, simulations, and field experiences.

7. The practical application of learning should be emphasized and related to the life-situations of the adult learners.

8. "The appropriate organizing principle for sequences of adult learning is *problem areas*, not *subjects*" (Knowles 1980, 54). Adult learners tend to be interested in and ready to solve problems: the starting point for instruction should be the problem or concern that adults have as they enter the educational setting. And subsequent activities should be centered on the problems or "tasks" that arise from these initial needs and diagnoses.

It is a serious and perhaps dangerous over-simplification to summarize the andragogy model in these brief lists. It must be remembered that the teaching and learning process is a complex one and that individual learners and groups of learners are very different from each other. No one rule or principle is likely to apply in every situation. Every attempt will be made to remind the reader of these complexities in subsequent chapters, while at the same time, providing clear and structured guidelines for the planning of instruction for adult learners. Meanwhile, for the inquiring and curious reader, the writings of Knowles listed in the bibliography are strongly recommended.

A necessary component of any process of theory-development is the analysis, application, and criticism of the ideas (or the explanation of the observations). Some research has been done on the assumptions of the andragogical model; much remains to be done. It is in no way to be considered as a proven theory, however influential on practice it has been. Other well-known writers have been critical of the ideas. Cross points out that the contrast between andragogy and pedagogy is "difficult to maintain" (Cross 1981, 223) and states that "we no longer have a theory of *adult* learning but, rather, a theory of instruction purporting to offer guidance to teachers in general" (Cross 1981, 223). Finally, she asks, "does andragogy lead to researchable questions that will advance knowledge in adult education?" (Cross 1981, 228) This is an essential criterion of a theory: we must be able to test it. Brookfield reminds us that "andragogy is also now, for many educators and trainers of adults, a badge of identity. Such individuals frequently describe themselves as 'andragogues,' declare that their practice exemplifies andragogical principles, and believe that the concept represents a professionally accurate summary of the unique characteristics of adult education practice" (Brookfield 1986, 90). He also specifically questions some of the underlying assumptions of andragogy: "There are good grounds, therefore, for maintaining that self-directedness—that is, autonomous control over aspects of work life, personal relationships, societal structures, and educational pursuits—is an empirical rarity" (Brookfield 1986, 94). And, "we must conclude, therefore, that while self-directedness is a desirable condition of human existence it is seldom found in any abundance" (Brookfield 1986, 94–95). Brookfield questions the problem-centered characteristic of the adult learner, quoting research which describes adults as "continually inquiring into new knowledge and skill domains whether or not these were related to some immediate life application" (Brookfield 1986, 99). He concludes this discussion by reminding us that the teaching and learning process is an exceedingly complex interaction, that "the concept is not at all as fixed or immutable as some practitioners might believe" (Brookfield 1986, 119).

While the profound influence of Knowles' writings on the field of adult education cannot be denied, the reflective practitioner must continue to question and experiment.

Theories of Learning

"There can be few intellectual quests that, for educators and trainers of adults, assume so much significance and yet contain so little promise of successful completion as the search for a general theory of adult learning" (Brookfield 1986, 25). Differences among individuals and the ways they best learn or prefer to learn are greater than any generalizable principles that have yet been developed. On the other hand, considerable valuable work has been done in describing how adults learn. It is the responsibility of practitioners and researchers to continually reflect on, analyze, and question this work. We cannot accept theories of learning or principles of adult learning as "givens" or as "laws" to be blindly acted upon.

Several theorists who have contributed to our understanding of how adults learn were not writing exclusively about adults. These works will be summarized briefly. Once again, the reader is referred to the original works listed in the bibliography for more information.

Gagné (1977) has described a model of learning relevant to individuals of all ages. He proposes that there are types of learning which form a hierarchy; that is, some types of learning must precede others. It is this notion of a hierarchy which has provided the foundation for much of instructional design. Gagné lists seven types of learning:

1. Stimulus-response learning, in which an individual responds to a situation or stimulus and the response is shaped by a reward;

2. Motor and verbal chaining, the learning of skills or rote (memorized) verbal learning;

3. Multiple discrimination, the intellectual skill of distinguishing among phenomena;

4. Concept learning, the understanding of abstract ideas;

5. Rule learning, in which an individual responds to a situation using rules;

6. Problem solving, in which the individual uses rules to find solutions to problems; and

7. Signal learning, which can occur at any level of the hierarchy, and is the association of a reward with a stimulus.

Gagné's (1977) discussion of the problem-solving cycle is another concept which has contributed to adult education. The problem-solving cycle includes: (1) the perception of a problem; (2) collection of observations, thoughts, and ideas about the problem; (3) formulation of hypotheses; (4) testing of hypotheses until a solution is found; (5) assimilation of the solution; and (6) the situation no longer perceived as a problem. The similarity to Dewey's work, described above, should be noted; many instructional strategies for adult learners are based on this model.

Mezirow (1977, 1981) contributed a unique and useful theoretical model of learning. Mezirow proposes that an individual learns when his or her perception of reality is "not in harmony with" experience. During a life "crisis" or dilemma (divorce, loss of job, promotion, relocation, etc.) an individual will experience this disharmony and will be receptive to learning. Mezirow (1981) describes a ten-step learning cycle:

1. a disorienting dilemma
2. self-examination
3. critical assessment and a sense of alienation
4. relating discontent to the experiences of others
5. exploring options for new ways of behaving
6. building confidence in new ways of behaving
7. planning a course of action
8. acquiring knowledge in order to implement plans
9. experimenting with new roles
10. reintegration into society

Mezirow also describes learning as "reflecting on experience" and elaborates on different levels of reflection, some of which he considers to be unique to the adult learner.

Carl Rogers (1969), a psychologist, has provided useful insights into the learning process, emphasizing the self-actualization of the learner as a goal of education. He described various characteristics of experiential learning which are now generally incorporated into theories of adult education:

1. The learner must perceive the relevance of the subject matter;
2. Learning involves a change in self-perception;
3. Learning occurs when the self is not threatened;
4. Learning is facilitated by doing;
5. Learning is facilitated when the learner actively participates in the process; and
6. Self-directed learning involves the whole person.

Brundage and Mackeracher undertook the integration of the voluminous research and writing on adult learning into a set of "learning principles" and their implications for educators. The complexity of this task is reflected in the nature and number of principles produced. After a considerable amount of analysis and synthesis, the authors provide a *summary* of 36 learning principles, each accompanied by implications for facilitating learning and implications for planning instruction. Examples of these principles are listed below; it is strongly recommended that the interested reader refer to the original document for the complete analysis.

Adults enter learning activities with an organized set of descriptions about themselves which influence their learning processes. The descriptions are the self-concept; the feelings are the self-esteem. Both are based on past experience and on how that experience was interpreted and valued by the learner (Brundage and Mackeracher 1980, 97).

Adult learning is facilitated when the learner's representation and interpretation of his own experiences are accepted as valid, acknowledged as an essential aspect influencing change, and respected as a potential resource for learning. The teacher can express positive regard for the learner and utilize the learner's past experience directly or indirectly in the teaching process (Brundage and Mackeracher 1980, 98).

Past experience presents the adult learner with a paradox in the learning situation. On the one hand, the stability of past experience and the learner's self-concept lead to confidence and a willingness to enter into the process of change. On the other hand, the process of change has the potential for changing the meanings, values, skills, and strategies of past experience and the self-concept, thereby temporarily destabilizing both. This lack of stability may lead to loss of confidence and to possible withdrawal from the process of change (Brundage and Mackeracher 1980, 101).

When adult learning focusses on the personal problems of an individual learner, the solutions to those problems must come from his own personal values and expectations, be implemented through his personal resources and skills, and be congruent with his personal meanings, strategies and life-style (Brundage and Mackeracher 1980, 103).

Some adult learning focusses on transforming the meanings, values, strategies, and skills derived from past experience. The act of transforming previous experience requires more time and energy than other types of learning. It also requires having a raised consciousness, reexamining figure-ground relationships, and redefining personal values and meanings, as well as testing new meanings, values, strategies and skills (Brundage and Mackeracher 1980, 104).

Adults do not learn productively when under severe time constraints. They tend to learn best when they can set their own pace. Their reduced speed is compensated for by improved efficiency and competence in learning strategies (Brundage and Mackeracher 1980, 108).

Adults learn best when they are in good health, are well rested, and are not experiencing stress (Brundage and Mackeracher 1980, 109).

Each adult learner has an individual learning style for effecting change in his or her behavior and an individual cognitive style for processing information. Each cognitive and learning style is effective and adaptive in some situations and ineffective in others (Brundage and Mackeracher 1980, 110).

This sample of Brundage and Mackeracher's learning principles demonstrates the complexity of the phenomenon with which we are dealing. At the same time, every reader can probably think of exceptions to each principle or argue that the list is not comprehensive. No set of principles or guidelines can be regarded as definitive. Each instructor of adults must question and adapt in each instructional situation.

On to Planning Instruction...

After such a description of the inadequacies and complexities of the theoretical foundations for planning instruction for adult learners, it may seem overly optimistic to describe a practical model for planning. However, regardless of the issues with which the theorists and researchers must grapple, the instructor faces a class next week, a workshop on Saturday, and a new group of learners or a new course next semester. As mentioned at the beginning of this chapter, an instructional design model has been chosen as the vehicle for planning, with every attempt made to incorporate what we know about adults as learners. The relevance of the instructional design model, as such, *can* be criticized. Brookfield (1986, 206) points out the discrepancy that usually exists between "texts on program development and the real world of practice" and addresses the "theory-practice disjunction" (Brookfield 1986, 202). Such issues must remain in our minds as we go about our daily planning and implementation of instruction; otherwise we become automatons of a system and lose track of our roles as *educators*.

CHAPTER TWO

CONSIDERING THE AUDIENCE

by Patricia Cranton and Cynthia B. Weston

Various terms are used to describe those for whom instruction is planned. They are often called the students, or the learners, and may sometimes be referred to as the audience or the target population. These terms can be used interchangeably. The options are provided because some individuals feel that the words "learner" and "student" sound school bound and therefore prefer to describe the recipients of instruction simply as an audience or target population. Regardless of the term used, those who will be on the receiving end of instruction must be considered from the beginning of the instructional planning process, since the educational background, intellectual characteristics, and affective characteristics of the audience will greatly affect how much and how well learning will occur.

Many instructors, in fact most instructors, intuitively size up their audience and make instructional decisions based upon that intuitive appraisal. Assume, for example, that the following objective, "the learner will be able to perform 10 tennis serves, placing 8 out of 10 into the designated service area," is designed for first year undergraduates in a Physical Education program. Several possible ways of teaching this skill to these students might immediately come to mind. Now suppose that the same skill will be taught to each of the following groups of students; individuals whose first language is Chinese, corporate executives, Inuit adults, your best friend's spouse, Olympic class swimmers, and young adults confined to wheelchairs. Undoubtedly, for each of the learner groups mentioned above, certain changes in the teaching method would be made based on assumptions about the learners' age, language ability, intellectual skills, physical skills, educational background, previous experience with the subject or related subjects, relationship to the instructor, and motivation level, to name a few.

Consideration of these various aspects of the learner is referred to as *audience analysis*. The learner is described, and often specific characteristics are investigated, by gathering information directly from individual members of the audience by means of questionnaires or tests. Results of analysis will aid in decision making at various points in the instructional design process. Analysis can be as simple or complex as the situation requires or as time allows, but it must be included as an essential step in any instructional planning.

In the following section, two aspects of audience analysis will be described: audience description and entry behaviors. A selected list of learner characteristics, which may be consulted during all phases of audience analysis, follows.

Audience Description

During the first stages of the instructional design process it is necessary to describe the audience for whom the instruction is intended. Most people usually begin by determining the learners':

- educational level
- age or age range
- prior knowledge of the subject
- previous experience
- mother tongue

Awareness of these learner characteristics will aid in determining the level of content, in sequencing instruction, and in selecting methods and materials. The description also often indicates any unusual characteristics which will influence the design of instruction, such as poor reading ability, or physical handicaps. This basic description provides adequate information on which to base preliminary instructional planning. If problems arise during the development of the instruction, it may be necessary to consider audience variables again to determine if there are any characteristics that are interacting with instructional materials and causing problems. Of course, there are many other areas that may be at fault when instruction fails, for example, poor sequencing, mismatch between objectives and evaluation, to name a few. However, one must always consider the audience characteristics, as well as instructional variables, when diagnosing instructional design weaknesses. Specific guidelines as to which audience characteristics should be investigated will not be given, as each instructional situation is unique. For your information and reference, many learner characteristics are described in the following pages, in fact, many more than any instructor would want to consider for any one course, or unit. The key word to remember in regard to audience analysis is *relevance*: the instructor should only consider or analyze those characteristics which are relevant to the instructional situation.

Entry Behaviors

Entry behaviors can be defined as the knowledge, skills, and abilities that learners bring to the instructional situation. We assume that university students are able to use language in reading, writing, and oral expression. While there is certainly a great deal of individual variation in proficiency in these skills, it would be fairly safe to say that verbal comprehension and expression are entry behaviors of university students. In this text, the term entry behaviors will be used to refer not only to the abilities that the learners bring to instruction but more specifically to what they *must* bring to instruction. Think of entry behaviors as prerequisites. Sometimes the learner characteristics that are described in the first part of audience analysis will also be a part of entry behaviors. One might describe the prior knowledge of the learners entering a statistics class on multiple regressions by saying that they all had passed a statistics class in analysis of variance. This would describe the prior knowledge of the audience. It might also be that the Analysis of Variance course is a prerequisite for the Multiple Regressions course. This would indicate an entry behavior, that is, one is required to have prior knowledge of analysis of variance techniques before beginning the Multiple Regressions course. Consideration of entry behaviors or prerequisites for instruction should be included in an audience analysis.

A commonly asked question is: "How much detail is necessary in specifying entry behaviors? Do I have to indicate that the students should be able to read and write?" The degree of detail will depend on the audience and the topic. Any prerequisite knowledge, skill, or ability that must be present for instruction to be effective and for objectives to be achieved, should be included in a statement of entry behaviors. Beware of the simplicity of this statement however, because too often the instructional designer overlooks obvious or simple behaviors which may be crucial to instructional sources. A well-designed biology unit that requires the use of a microscope will not succeed if the learners do not know how to use a microscope. If they must use a microscope as part of the learning experience, then either the students must already be able to use one properly, or instruction in its use must be included as part of the unit or course.

The assessment of entry behaviors may be done informally or formally. Ability to use a microscope might be informally determined by questioning participants orally or by asking them to demonstrate its use. More formal assessment procedures may, however, be necessary in some situations. A college chemistry instructor could require the learners to pass a test in which they had to describe and demonstrate, with a mock up, safe use of the Bunsen burner before they were allowed to use the real thing. One would certainly hope that the entry behaviors of dentists and pilots in training had been formally assessed before they were allowed to practice skills on the unsuspecting public. This formal assessment before instruction is often referred to as *pretesting*.

The learner characteristics in the following section may be helpful in your consideration of entry behaviors. Once again, remember that one should not attempt to assess as many characteristics as possible, but should only consider those which are relevant to instruction.

Learner Characteristics

The adult education literature (cf. Brookfield, 1986; Brundage & Mackeracher, 1980; Knowles, 1980) describes the general characteristics of the adult learner. The commonly discussed characteristics will be summarized.

Most often, adults become involved in a learning situation by choice (an obvious exception would be mandatory professional development or in-service work). Since the adult has *chosen* to learn, he will have clear and specific goals related to his own needs, whether it be an improvement in job skills or a desire for social contact. The adult learners will expect the instructional situation to be relevant to their needs.

Adults enter a learning situation with a variety of life *experiences*. The older the learners, the more experience they bring and the more varied it will be in any one group. Learning is facilitated when the instruction is related to these experiences.

Most adults have concrete *immediate* goals. They have taken a course or attended a workshop in order to learn a specific skill or have a certain set of questions addressed. They will have little patience with the instructor's idea of what is "important" for them to learn.

Usually, adults prefer to be *self-directed* learners. They do not want to be treated like children and told what to do. Since they have their own goals and experiences, they want to find activities and ways of doing things that relate to them. They have established preferences for working alone, in groups, by listening, by reading, by doing. However, adults in a new learning situation or adults returning to "school" after many years will be anxious or uncomfortable and will likely demonstrate dependent behaviors. Introducing self-directed learning will only further increase that anxiety and discomfort. Knowles (1980) describes one role of the adult educator as a facilitator of independent, self-directed learning (i.e. the adult learner is gradually encouraged to become self-directed).

Older adult learners have unique *physical requirements*. They need more light, more "breaks" in order to stretch, comfortable chairs, perhaps larger print on the flip chart, and louder volume on the tape. They may need more time to perform certain tasks.

Adults may have *rigid* values, opinions, or behaviors. Also, their values, opinions, and thoughts must be respected. This again leads the instructor of adults to the role of facilitator rather than that of formal authority or expert.

Adults with a positive *self-concept* are likely to be better learners, although the return to an instructional situation may be perceived as threatening and have a negative effect on self-concept. The environment, therefore, must be designed to foster a positive self-image.

The difficulty, of course, with general characteristics of the adult learner is that they may not be relevant to any one adult or any one group of adults. Adults are probably more *different* from each other than children, by virtue of having lived longer and having undergone more variety of experiences. The instructor of adults must consider the audience for whom the planning is being done.

The characteristics to be considered will be described under four main categories: educational background, intellectual characteristics and abilities, affective/personality characteristics, and perceptual/motor characteristics and abilities. Some aspects of learners, such as age and sex, which are difficult to place in any category since they are inextricably related to all, will be discussed separately at the outset. This particular presentation of audience characteristics is somewhat arbitrary and is primarily a convenient way for organizing a multiplicity of individual factors that can and do affect what is learned from the planned instruction. The list of possible characteristics that could be included is awesome; therefore this section presents only a selection of some of the most common learner attributes. Techniques for gathering information about the various attributes are presented when possible, though the use of any particular measure is not necessarily advocated. Those aspects of the audience that seem relevant should be considered, using any techniques that render useful information to the instructor.

Age

When describing an individual to someone else, one of the first things often mentioned is age. Age gives an indication of someone's appearance and experience, among other things. When planning instruction, age is also one of the things an instructor considers. Needless to say, if the purpose of instruction is to explore Impressionist techniques, the topic would probably be approached quite differently with individuals 18 years of age than with those 50 years of age. Chronological age can be an important factor to consider; however a statement of age only renders very general information since ten individuals who are 30 years old may be completely different in every other respect. A consideration of their age may suggest a level of content and vocabulary that will be appropriate for the learners, or the types of examples and activities that may be relevant and motivating to the learners. Age can also be a very misleading and erroneous factor on which to base instructional decisions, and therefore should always be coupled with other information about the learners. (The relationship of age to intellectual development is more fully discussed in the section on intellectual abilities.) A gifted or talented individual may be far advanced when compared to other individuals of the same age. Handicapped adults cannot be taught in the same way that college graduates are taught. Providing equivalent instruction to individuals based solely upon consideration of age may not lead to effective learning and, in fact, can lead to instructional disaster.

Gender

Great pains are taken today to avoid discrimination on the basis of gender, which might suggest that instruction should be handled identically for any audience, for any subject. There are some subjects which may be more relevant to one sex than the other, for example, rape, abortion, fathering, or self-examination of the breast. This does not necessarily mean that the topic of abortion should be handled differently for a male audience than for a female audience, but it very well could be without being considered sexist.

Most instructors find themselves teaching mixed audiences. When designing instruction for such groups, it is desirable to avoid stereotypical examples such as the male doctor, the female nurse; the male dentist, the female assistant; the male executive, the female secretary. Use of such examples not only reinforces sexual stereotypes, but also can alienate members of the audience. It is also desirable to use examples calculated to appeal to both the men and women in the audience. A specific example may serve to demonstrate this point. Each year students about to embark on student teaching experience prepare materials to use in the field. A physical educational student-instructor wanted to design a poster intended to encourage her class to become involved in a weight-training program. She dutifully considered the intended audience and indicated that they were 18 to 21 years old, physically active males and females. With objective in hand and some basic audience characteristics in mind, she went off to create her materials. Seeking a second opinion about the appropriateness of the materials, she brought in the poster. It was bold and attractive, but the pictures showed only men, approximately 30 years old, weighing close to 250 pounds, struggling to lift and press enormous amounts of weight. Considering that her intended audience was composed of males and females, 18 to 21 years old, the efficacy of the materials had to be questioned. These materials were not the most motivating models for the intended audience. Only picturing men might lead women to believe that this was not a course intended for them. Both males and females might be discouraged from taking the course if they thought they would end up looking like those hefty fellows. And as the pictured models were quite a bit older, the impression might be created that the course was not for their age group. It would have been more appropriate to use pictures of people similar in age and sex to the intended audience.

Fleming and Levie (1981) in their book *Instructional Message Design*, provide principles from research in the behavioral sciences that can be considered when designing instruction. One principle, among many, that is particularly relevant to this discussion, states that if the receiver (the audience) and the source (the poster) are similar, communication and acceptance of the message will be enhanced. This principle is applicable to the design of all aspects of instruction.

Educational Background

There are a number of learner characteristics which can be discussed under the general heading of educational background. Education is interpreted in its broadest sense to include attributes that are a product of informal as well as formal learning.

a) Language. It is essential to determine whether the learners can understand and communicate in the language of instruction. Foreign language classes are an obvious exception. In North America it is not uncommon to find that some or many learners in a group do not share the same mother tongue. There seem to be at least two schools of thought on this issue. One position asserts that learners attending a French, English, Hispanic, German, Greek, etc., session should be expected to perform and be evaluated in the language of instruction. No concession is made, otherwise the standards associated with the instruction would be compromised. The other position assumes that education or learning in other than one's mother tongue may present difficulties to the learner, for example, when being formally evaluated or when reading advanced materials. Perhaps, consideration should be extended to the second language learners by extending deadlines (where relevant), finding alternative readings, or even arranging some activities in the language of preference. Obviously this decision depends on the nature of the instructional situation. In professional education, the participants' facility with language would be crucial; in a general interest, non-credit situation, it would not be as relevant.

The instructor will wish to determine language ability and decide what considerations will be made. If proficiency in a particular language is essential then it should be stated as an entry behavior.

b) Educational level. Many instructors want to know the age of the learners, assuming that age will give them an indication of the learner's level and ability. Often what the instructor is really after is the educational level of the audience. Are they high school graduates, undergraduates, graduate students, or continuing education students? Or, have the workshop participants completed other courses on the topic or attended other workshops? Information about general educational level will provide some basic information about prior knowledge or skills, reading level, anxiety about being a learner, and so on. However, it is a very rough descriptor of the audience.

c) Prior knowledge. Previous organized study and learning in a subject area is referred to as prior knowledge. If a learner has prior knowledge of a subject area, then there is a base of information on which subsequent instruction can build. Very often prior knowledge of some kind is required as an entry behavior.

Assessing a learner's prior knowledge of the topic or content will assist in determining level and inclusiveness of the topic as well as in selecting methods and materials. Assessment is commonly done in many formal and informal ways. Adults registering for a French course, for example, often are asked if they have taken previous French courses and if so when, how many, etc. They may be asked to take a test which will help to determine their current ability so that they can be placed in a level that will be most appropriate for their current abilities.

Whether there has been formal pretesting or a more informal assessment, determination of prior knowledge will help not only in selecting the appropriate level of content, but can help also in selecting methods and materials for instruction. It can generally be said that the more basic the level of knowledge in a content area, the more desirable it is to use methods and materials that provide concrete experience and examples. As the level of knowledge becomes more advanced and sophisticated, methods and materials of a more abstract nature can be used. This is discussed in more depth in the chapter on methods and materials.

d) Previous experience. As mentioned before, adult learners may have gained experience in a subject area in a variety of informal ways, such as learning a language just by living in a foreign country, learning a skill on the job, or learning about medicine by talking with physician friends about their work. Individuals may have a great deal of experience gained by years of playing hockey or speaking a language; however, they may also make a multitude of errors or have various misconceptions about the topic. The term "previous experience" connotes familiarity with, but not necessarily organized knowledge about, a subject. Frequently, previous experience, particularly that gained in a practical setting, is just as valuable and even more effective than organized study.

Determination of previous experience can be done informally by requiring the learners to demonstrate their ability in some way. Previous experience may affect the level of instruction as well as the sequence, methods, and materials. It is neither necessary nor fruitful to require the audience to attend to something that has already been learned through experience. Instead, one should relate the instruction to the learners' experiences with the subject.

e) Past Academic Achievement. Some consideration of learner achievement in previous courses can provide useful information. Most instructors are faced with heterogeneous groups. There are no easy formulas for designing instruction for groups with mixed academic background or ability. Recognition that the students have varied in the levels of academic achievement usually means that the instructor must work to reach all students by using a variety of methods and materials. As will be discussed in upcoming sections on cognitive style and learning style, achievement may be linked to a great number of factors other than intellectual ability.

Finding out about a learner's past academic record also has some disadvantages. You may develop expectations which can bias your perception of the individual's performance or even affect the learning. There are many examples of this in educational literature. Instructors hear that they are getting a poor student and proceed to find the student's work poor, because this is what they are expecting. On the other hand, an instructor who is unaware of a poor past record may foster that individual's self-concept and confidence which may lead to much needed success. Any findings regarding past academic achievement should be used with caution.

Intellectual Characteristics

Describing the intellectual characteristics of the audience is probably one of the most difficult aspects of audience analysis. Familiarity with the intellectual skills and abilities of the learners will aid in determining such things as the pace of instruction, selection of vocabulary, and the appropriate level of abstraction or concreteness of content presentation. Intellectual characteristics will be considered from several perspectives.

Once again, keep in mind that these are guidelines only, not strict criteria for decision making.

a) Reading ability. Standard measures are available which can be used to determine reading vocabulary, speed, and comprehension. Use of this information will vary depending upon the objectives of the instruction.

Assume that the objective is: "The learners will select three adjectives that describe the personality of Queen Elizabeth I and support these choices by describing an event from her life in which these characteristics were manifested." The learners are known to have poor reading ability. Several methods could be used to present information related to this objective: reading about Elizabeth I, hearing about her, watching a media production or a play about her, to name a few. If this is a general interest course, the instructor may be concerned that the students achieve the objective and not necessarily be concerned about the manner in which the relevant information is acquired. In this case, it would probably be best to pursue the objective via the path of least resistance—in some manner other than reading, or by providing reading materials that are simple enough for the learners, coupled with some information presentation techniques. Conversely, if this is a course primarily designed to increase students' reading skills, it would be desirable to choose reading as the mode of information presentation, starting with materials written at a level equivalent to learner abilities and gradually increasing difficulty, thereby stretching the student. If it is a required English history course, it would be desirable to use a combination of instructional methods and materials so that the learning is challenging but not frustrating, in that it does not emphasize reading only, where the students are weak, but may capitalize on other abilities.

b) Intellectual development. According to developmental theorists, such as Piaget and Bruner, the intellect evolves through stages or levels, each stage being characterized by increasingly complex intellectual abilities. While the sequence is fixed (in other words, an individual must pass through one stage before moving on to the next), the speed with which one moves from stage to stage varies considerably.

Bruner (1968) describes three stages of development which roughly correspond to Piaget's (1929) four levels of development. Piaget and Bruner agree that learning is facilitated if learners are provided with instruction that is of a form comparable to that at their level of intellectual development. In other words, if dealing with learners at the iconic level, it is necessary to provide concrete objects and activities that will allow them to acquire new information in a manner that matches their intellectual development. For learners 15 years and older, who should ostensibly be operating at a symbolic intellectual level, it is probable that the instructor could deal exclusively with abstract symbols. This is not always the case, as there is a great range in symbolic abilities and the age at which one develops these abilities. Deaf adults, for example, often do not pass into the symbolic stage of intellectual development until well after the age of 15. Additionally, recent research has indicated that while adults may be operating at the symbolic level in one subject area, such as English, they may not have developed the same intellectual ability in mathematics.

When faced with a class of unknown intellectual levels (there are measures available for determining intellectual development), it would be wise to provide concrete referents before moving on to abstractions and abstract relationships. Concrete referents can be provided in the form of real things and examples which relate to the experience of the audience. Additionally, providing context by relating new ideas to previous learning and previous experience will allow the learners to approach new learning from an established base.

c) Cognitive styles. It has been determined that there are differences in the ways that individuals acquire, process, store, and use information. These intellectual idiosyncracies are referred to as cognitive style. A person's cognitive style is not a single feature but a combination of many traits or dimensions.

Many dimensions of cognitive style have been investigated. Those which have received the most attention will be described, along with assessment procedures that are available for measuring individual functioning in a particular dimension. In some cases, standardized measures have been developed, and in other cases, a variety of nonstandardized tests are available. For other traits, there is controversy as to whether the dimension can be measured at all, since there seem to be other cognitive functions which may influence results.

1. Field independence/field dependence. This dimension refers to an individual's ability to separate embedded items from a complex context, for example, to separate details from a larger scene. One of the procedures used to assess in individual's field independence/dependence is the Embedded Figure Tests (EFT), which require the viewer to locate simple figures in a more complex figure. Those who are able to find the simple figures are said to be field independent, meaning that they can overcome the complexity of the background (the "field") in order to see smaller, simple figures that are included or embedded within that field. Those who cannot separate the embedded figures are said to be field dependent. One's functioning in this dimension is often related to more pervasive personality characteristics: a field independent person tends to be better at analytical tasks, and a field dependent person tends to be better at more global, social tasks.

2. Reflectivity/Impulsivity. Classification on this dimension is based primarily upon one's speed of response to a task such as problem solving. The most common measure of this dimension is the Matching Familiar Figures (MFF) test, wherein the individual is asked to match a given figure with one of several alternatives that are presented simultaneously. An impulsive individual responds quickly and often incorrectly; the reflective individual ponders the various alternatives, responding slowly and usually accurately.

The tendency to be reflective or impulsive once again seems to be linked to personality attributes which may be influenced by two somewhat conflicting social demands: (1) get the right answer and (2) get it fast. The impulsive person, who feels it is most important to have quick success, responds rapidly and therefore is often labeled a high risk individual. Reflective individuals are low risk; they feel that it is important to get the correct answer, to do it right, and in an effort to avoid failure, carefully consider all alternatives.

3. Conceptualizing styles. This dimension refers to individual differences in the tendency to categorize perceived similarities and differences among stimuli. There is not a standardized test for measuring this dimension of cognitive style; however several measures are available, all of which are similar in that they require the individual to sort items into categories. The individual is not provided with any predetermined categories and therefore must survey all the items, determine commonalities and differences, and ultimately categorize them according to these perceived attributes. Individuals apparently exhibit categorizing strategies which have been labeled (a) conservative focusing and (b) focus gambling. In the former, the individual uses one example of a concept as the focus, changes one attribute of other examples, one at a time, until essential or common attributes are determined. One who uses focus gambling strategy also selects a focus example but changes more than one attribute at a time when searching for essential features.

4. Breadth of categorizing. This dimension concerns the individual tendency toward broad inclusiveness or narrow exclusiveness when categorizing items. Various tests are used to determine one's breadth of categorizing style. They usually provide the individual with one or several categories and a selection of items which must be purposively included or excluded from the categories. A person who tends to make inclusion errors, by placing items in inappropriate categories, is classified as a broad categorizer. One who makes exclusion errors, by failing to place items in appropriate categories, is a narrow categorizer. There may be some links here with reflective (low risk) and impulsive (high risk) traits.

5. Constricted vs. Flexible Control. This dimension concerns individual differences in susceptibility to distraction and cognitive interference. Some individuals are more prone to be distracted from a task than are others. Using measures such as the Stroop Color Word Test (for adults), an individual involved in performing a task is presented with potential distraction. Those who can ignore the interference and continue to focus on the task have flexible control. Those who are distracted are classified as having constricted control.

6. Leveling vs. Sharpening. There appear to be individual variations in assimilation of memory, that is, the way new stimuli are integrated into existing memories. Some individuals exhibit a tendency to level or blur and merge new stimuli with previous recollections and experience that are similar but not identical. Other individuals exhibit a tendency to sharpen which, at the other extreme, means they perceive new stimuli as less similar to previous experience than they really are. Tests associated with measurement of this dimension require the individual to remember a sequence of gradually changing stimuli. Those who retain discrete images are sharpeners; those who produce an undifferentiated recollection are levelers. Controversy surrounds the measure of this dimension of cognitive style since some researchers feel that memory functioning is confounded by other individual differences.

7. Cognitive Complexity/Simplicity. Investigation of this dimension tends to indicate that individuals differ in their tendency to construe the world, especially the world of social behavior, in a multi-dimensional way. Persons high in complexity are able to integrate information into an existing hierarchy and be more discriminating. This is another aspect of cognitive style which is surrounded by controversy, primarily concerning measurement. The Role Construct Repertory is one of the tests used to assess functioning on this dimension.

8. Visual/Haptic Perceptual Type is a dimension which concerns preferences for learning either through visual or kinesthetic senses. Visuals prefer to use the eyes for acquiring information. Haptics prefer to gather information through kinesthetic and physical means, for example, they learn and remember something better when they do it, than if they read or are told about it.

There are no rights or wrongs in terms of cognitive style, no intelligent styles; there are merely differences. The various dimensions of cognitive style are important audience characteristics because they influence the learners' ability to acquire, process, store, and use the information presented in instruction.

An area of related research has been concerned with Aptitude Treatment Interaction (ATI), which investigates the relationship between aptitudes (the various dimensions of cognitive style) and treatments (the instructional method or technique). It has been found that there are often interactions between cognitive style and instruction so that two individuals with different cognitive styles may learn different amounts from the same instruction. A common example is the interaction of field independence and IQ tests. It has been found that field independent individuals consistently test as more intelligent than field dependents. Their ability to separate details from complex information may be one of the factors of success rather than intelligence.

Related to ATI, Clark (1975) has recently suggested a procedure which may help the instructor minimize any mismatch between cognitive style and instructional task. He suggests three steps in designing instruction. The first step is to go back to the task analysis and carefully consider the requirements of each task, for example, will the learner be required to separate specific items from a group of stimuli (field dependence/independence) in order to analyze components, or be required to remember a string of items (levelling vs. sharpening) for comparison. It will be recalled that these tasks are easy for some learners and difficult for some, depending on their cognitive style. The second step is to determine which learners have the required abilities in terms of cognitive style. For those who do not have the required abilities, assistance will be necessary in order to perform the task as designed. Rather than redesign the task for each individual, a laudable but generally unrealistic approach, Clark suggests a third step of determining how to provide supplantation (which for now can be thought of as remediation) for those learners with an incongruent style. Research is necessary before a set of supplantation guidelines can be offered. For the present, the instructor can perform this kind of task/learner analysis in order to determine task requirements that present difficulty to individuals with particular cognitive styles. The instructor can remove the difficulty either by altering the mode of presentation of the task or performing (through supplantation) the task for the learner. Supplantation techniques which can be provided with various media will be discussed in the chapter on methods and material. One example of successful supplantation is provided in a classic study by Salomon (1974). Students were required to pick details out of a painting. Field dependent individuals were unable to do this. During a training phase, their inability was supplanted with the use of a video camera that zoomed in on required details. In a follow-up test, the same field dependents were able to separate details from a complex field. The supplantation training was apparently successful.

Affective/Personality Characteristics

Audience attitudes, values, opinions, beliefs, interests, and preferences can influence learning as such, and perhaps are more important than intellectual characteristics. It is artificial to treat intellectual and affective characteristics as discrete units; however, for the purposes of this discussion, it is necessary to separate individual variables in a way that facilitates audience analysis.

Motivation. Certainly every instructor will agree that such things as motivation and interest can have greater impact on learning than cognitive abilities. A classic example of this is the learner of a second language who struggles with grammar and vocabulary in a classroom setting but can acquire an astonishing vocabulary, full of subtle nuances, in a few hours with friends. Other individuals can't remember the names or functions of current provincial Members of Parliament but know every baseball player in the National League, along with their batting averages and professional and amateur backgrounds. Motivation is a key ingredient in a learning situation.

Motivation is that which arouses, sustains, and directs attention. It affects not only attention, but also remembering, forgetting, learning, and performance. Motivation is affected by many factors—abilities, needs, educational goals, fears, habits, skills, and socioeconomic status. Consider the relationship between cognitive abilities and motivation. In the preceding discussion of reading ability it was stated that if the instructor is faced with a group of poor readers, information should be represented either in a written form that matches reader abilities or via other channels. This technique avoids frustrating the audience and thwarting motivation. Even the most motivated among us would become discouraged if we consistently failed at a task.

A learner can be motivated by intrinsic or extrinsic forces. The intrinsically motivated individual wants to learn because of internal needs, desires, or goals. In other cases, extrinsic or external motivators, such as a promotion at work or reinforcement from colleagues or family, may encourage the individual to pursue the learning task.

One of the first tasks of the instructor is to determine the motivation of the audience. As mentioned earlier, many adult audiences have chosen to participate in the situation and have immediate goals. Instruction which is relevant to the learner needs will result in a motivated audience. Motivation can be stimulated by artificial factors such as rewards, but those activities and approaches that will be interesting to the learners must be determined. Ultimately the goal of the educator should be to develop intrinsic motivation in learners.

One might assume that if motivation is so important in learning, the greater the motivation, the greater the learning. This is not necessarily true. The Yerkes-Dodson law states that the ideal motivation level decreases with the difficulty of the task. So if the task is simple, high motivation is fine, but if the task is complex an excess of motivation might actually impede learning.

Anxiety. Anxiety is an apprehension, uneasiness, or agitation about some...well, here a problem arises. Anxiety often has no definable object. It is often apprehension of some vague, abstract event or contingency. Individuals range from highly anxious (the worrywart) to hardly anxious (Mr. Cool). A person's anxiety level has an effect on learning and performance. A little anxiety can be motivating, but too much anxiety can be crippling.

There are several questionnaires available which help to determine an individual's level of anxiety, in relation to tests, for example, the Test Anxiety Scale and the Achievement Anxiety Test (Alpert & Haber 1960). When instruction includes testing, it should be recognized that many high anxiety adults will perform poorly because of irrelevant responses to the test itself, such as worrying about failure or blocking on questions. This becomes particularly important in courses where the only evaluation of learning or feedback is through responses to a test. The high test anxiety learner may be comfortable with the material but will be consistently penalized by the system which places him or her in an anxiety producing situation. Place this person in a less threatening situation, and performance will improve. Low test anxiety individuals, on the other hand, often excel in tests because they find the situation challenging and look forward to assessment.

Anxiety should not necessarily be avoided as it can be stimulating to all learners. Even high anxiety learners report that apprehension acts in two ways—facilitation (improves performance) and debilitation (interferes with performance). Several guidelines can be offered to the instructor: anxious students do less well in high stress situations (McKeachie, 1978); anxiety tends to be increased by uncertainty, therefore anxious individuals work more effectively in highly structured situations (McKeachie, 1978); high anxiety learners perform better in an instructor-centered approach, while low anxiety individuals perform better when the learning is self-directed (Domino, 1975).

Internal/External Locus of Control. An aspect of personality which has received a great deal of attention is locus of control. It describes the degree to which individuals believe that they have control over their environment. It also describes the causes to which successes or failures are attributed. A person with internal locus of control feels directly responsible for his or her own success or failure. One with external locus of control perceives the self as powerless and attributes success or failure to luck, fate, or other powerful individuals. "Internals" seem to be more self-confident and self-controlled and are more active in trying to control situations which affect them. As with motivation, there seems to be a link between socioeconomic status and locus of control. Upper class individuals tend to be internally controlled, while lower class individuals are often external. The explanation given for this is that lower class individuals feel that they have little access to power and limited social mobility.

"Externals" seem to learn less as they perceive little relationship between their behavior and reward or reinforcement. Since they feel that fate is responsible for outcomes, they use time poorly in test-taking situations and consequently perform poorly. "Internals" use time more efficiently and generally perform better. The instructor may wish to assess locus of control. (This can be done by using a questionnaire developed by Rotter (1966).) Unfortunately, techniques for modifying locus of control have not been firmly established.

Learning Styles. Cognitive style, an aspect of intellectual characteristics of the learner, was defined as the way we acquire, process, store, and use information. Learning styles, in contrast, are affective and personality characteristics which affect our *preferences* for learning conditions. An example may help to clarify what is meant by learning style. You like to eat and probably will continue to eat all of your life. One of your preferred foods is chocolate cake which you eat often and with great enjoyment. In fact, you may even go out of your way to find a good piece of chocolate cake. In the absence of your favorite food and in the face of enormous hunger, you would probably eat mashed turnips, even though you do not particularly care for them. So it is with learning. (Whoever said it was a piece of cake?) Individuals can learn in situations that conflict with personal preferences (that's the turnips), but they may not learn as much, as well, or as enjoyably as they will in their preferred conditions (that's the cake).

Learning style, like cognitive style, is not a single feature but is composed of many dimensions. Dunn and Dunn (1977) have developed a structure which conveniently organizes preferred learning conditions into four categories: immediate environment, sociological needs, physical needs, and emotional aspects.

1. Immediate environment. When working on new or difficult tasks, individuals have definite preferences for environmental conditions. There are at least four environmental factors which can be manipulated to match learner style—sound, light, temperature, and design. Consider your own preferences. Do you like to read with music playing or in silence; with bright lights or in subdued lighting; in a warm room or a cool place; sitting on a hard chair at a desk or lying on a couch? It is erroneous to believe that all "serious" learners work in a nice quiet room, sitting at a desk, with bright lights. Whatever your preference, you can be sure to find among your colleagues and friends those who would become distracted and disinterested in the environment that you find the most conducive to study.

2. Sociological need. In this category are included several combinations of learning relationships: working with peers, alone, in pairs, or in groups. These preferences not only reflect independence needs, but also involve instructor-learner relationships. Some individuals (e.g. high anxiety) prefer to learn from or with the instructor while others do much better when working with peers.

3. Physical needs. Included here are perceptual strengths, intake needs, time of day, and mobility. The concept of perceptual strengths, as used here, does not refer to the way we choose to approach information but rather to the optimal way in which we process information. These strengths are often similar because, as living organisms, we have a tendency to select and develop techniques for learning that are most effective. However, it is possible for an individual to consistently select a perceptual mode that does not produce the most effective learning. Regarding intake needs, some people like to eat or drink while working, and others prefer to fast. The optimal time of day for study and work also varies greatly—from early in the morning to very late at night. Finally, the need for mobility, or moving around, differs for individuals involved in learning tasks. Some like to sit in one place all day without moving, while others jump up and down to pace the floor or to get endless cups of coffee (intake need).

4. Emotional aspects. Included in this category are motivation, persistence, responsibility, and need for structure. Once again, individual behavior varies greatly according to the amount of motivation, persistence, and responsibility a learner feels toward the learning task. Structure refers to an individual's preference to work with imposed deadlines or to work at a measured pace. It is not uncommon to find opposing styles in equally successful individuals: "I work best under pressure," and "I like to take my time and get things done in advance." There are obvious relationships between intellectual and affective learner characteristics. The human being is a complex organism that cannot easily be partitioned into discrete categories. The beauty of learning styles though, as confounded as they may be with other audience characteristics, is that so many of these factors can be easily manipulated and controlled to allow for variability in learner preference. Dunn and Dunn's Learning Style Inventory (1977) can be administered in order to determine learner preference. There are other inventories that can be used as well, though they reflect somewhat different conceptions of learning style. The energetic instructor can then set about creating options in terms of the environment, social conditions, and situations that allow for various physical needs, as well as creating flexible or structured schedules for individual learners.

Considering learner characteristics clearly creates more work for the instructor if action is to be taken based on findings. Undoubtedly, this is one reason that the topic is avoided. It is much easier to plan instruction in a simple, uniform manner, rather than to think of addressing differences in learners. It is not surprising to find that teaching style often reflects personal cognitive and learning styles, which means that many learners are being approached in a way that is undoubtedly a lot like turnips. Here, in the matter of learning conditions, are some concrete options which will begin to capitalize on learner differences to make for more effective learning. Since these affective characteristics are present in every educational and instructional situation, they should be considered when planning instruction.

Perceptual and Motor Characteristics

The final category of learner characteristics concerns the area of physical and psychomotor abilities. As with cognitive and affective characteristics, this is not really a discrete category but rather another perspective from which the learner can be viewed.

It might appear that perceptual and motor characteristics would be of concern only to the instructor involved with Physical Education or other areas which obviously require physical coordination. However, every instructional situation relies on an individual's ability to perceive, most commonly through visual and auditory channels. Much cognitive learning and behavior must occur in conjunction with perceptual and motor activity. Reading, for example, requires visual perceptual ability before information can be processed. Written communication requires fine motor coordination. Motor abilities are required for spoken and gestural language. In the trades, manual dexterity is required for tool usage. Fine arts require a great deal of perceptual and motor skill for painting, singing, or using musical instruments.

As with other learner characteristics, perceptual and motor factors are considered when analyzing the audience. This category is most commonly included in audience description when there are handicaps which may affect the selection of methods or materials: for example, blind learners will not benefit from visual presentation; auditory materials are not usually appropriate for deaf students; activities may need modification if students are in wheelchairs; a student with cerebral palsy may have limited control of hand movement, which would require modification of tasks which call for fine motor skills. Specific perceptual and motor skills are often required to assure that the learner has the necessary abilities upon which to build further skills, such as demonstration of basic skiing ability before entering a second-level course. In other situations, a demonstration of skills may be used as a selection device for determining who has the competencies necessary to pursue a particular vocation. For example, finger dexterity, as measured by a manual manipulation task, is a necessary skill for an individual entering the dental profession. It will not always be necessary to describe perceptual/motor characteristics or entry behaviors of the audience. Consideration of these factors should be included when there is a handicap or when it is otherwise relevant to the instruction. It is important to make a distinction between perceptual abilities and psychomotor abilities.

a) **Perceptual abilities.** Perception refers to our ability to make sense out of the visual, auditory, gustatory (taste), olfactory (smell), and tactile stimuli we receive. Individuals vary greatly in perceptual abilities. A sensory handicap, such as visual or auditory impairment, interferes with ability to perceive. There are also various kinds of perceptual handicaps in which the sensory organs and receptors seem to be in working order, but some problem along the way interferes with ability to make sense out of sensory stimuli and/or to produce a meaningful response. Some individuals appear to have unusual perceptual abilities, such as the wine taster's ability to detect fine differences among wines. They may not necessarily have more sensitive tongues or noses, but they do have unusual ability to perceive differences.

It is not possible here to delve into the details of where sensory reception ends and perception begins or where perception ends and cognition begins. The purpose of this initial discussion is to emphasize that sensory and perceptual abilities play an important role in learning. Compensation can be made for sensory impairments particularly through the selection and design of appropriate instructional methods and materials.

b) Motor abilities. If you think of perception as the input or incoming phase of a process, motor skills can be thought of as one of the outputs or responses to sensation, perception, and cognition. Fleishman (1964) considers physical abilities in five broad categories: strength, flexibility-speed, balance, coordination, and endurance. A variety of instructional situations might require proficiency in one or more of these areas, as an entry behavior. (For example, individuals in an advanced weight-lifting class must have strength.) Fleishman also separates five manipulative skills into seven dimensions: control precision, multilimbs coordination, response orientation, reaction time, speed of arm-hand steadiness, wrist-finger speed, and aiming. If one of these skills is required in order for the learner to be successful in instruction, then it should be an entry behavior, or its development should be included in instruction.

Summary

Planning for or adapting to the seemingly endless variety of learner characteristics is probably the most difficult task faced by the instructor of adults. An example that is probably fairly typical comes to mind. A recent convert to the principles of adult education was preparing to work with a group of new college instructors in an Instructor Training Program. In her planning, she used the general characteristics of adult learners as a guide to the characteristics of her audience and planned self-directed activities, independent projects, and group work. In reality, the instructors were frightened of the situation; they came from a wide variety of backgrounds, including the trades, technologies, and academic areas; and they wanted to be told what to do. They wanted support, guidance, structure, practical hints, and *authority*. After a disastrous first two days, the instructor knew that she had to go back to pedagogical techniques for a while; by the third week of the intensive program, the participants were happily working on their own or in groups and producing remarkable work.

But how does the adult educator know how to plan? The most important consideration may well be an *awareness* of the variety of individuals who could be in any one instructional situation. And then, the willingness to throw plans away and start over again after the first few hours spent with the audience. Whenever it is possible to collect advance information about the audience, it is strongly recommended that this be done. A questionnaire can be sent out with registration. Colleagues can be consulted. The first session can be devoted to collecting information and getting to know the audience. Often none of this is practical—a one-day workshop with an unknown group does not always allow a "needs assessment" to be done. At that point, it becomes a matter of being perceptive and flexible, of asking and listening to the answers, and of being prepared to change your plans.

The instructor of adults who has years of experience will still sometimes misjudge an audience or not have the resources to adapt to a specific audience. There can be no set of rules that will take the instructor through this process. If a general rule were to be stated, it would be that a *variety* of methods and materials should be planned so that different individuals with different preferences and abilities would feel satisfied with some aspects of the situation. When the audience is mature or independent, developing optional activities, projects, and materials may be the best strategy.

CHAPTER THREE

OBJECTIVES

An objective is simply a statement of what participants are expected to learn or be able to do after the instruction. When an instructor compiles a list of topics for a course outline or selects readings or activities, this is an implicit statement of objectives. Translating such a list into clearly worded statements of what the learner will be able to do has several advantages, from both the learners' and the instructor's perspectives.

When the instructor compiles a list of objectives or when the instructor and the participants agree on a set of objectives, the methods, materials, and evaluation or feedback techniques can be clearly related to those objectives. The learner is aware of expectations. The information acts as a guide in focussing on relevant points during instruction, in reading, in completing activities or assignments, and in providing feedback or evaluating participants' performance. We have all experienced the frustration of being in a class with no idea of what the important concepts are and therefore attempting to out-guess the instructor at evaluation time. The use of objectives helps to overcome such an unproductive instructional situation.

For the instructor, objectives become an invaluable aid in the planning process. The selection of teaching methods and materials is greatly facilitated by clear statements of expected learning. The feedback and evaluation process becomes a much more straightforward procedure. If, for example, an objective in an introductory psychology course is, "The learner will be able to define and give examples of behavior for each of Piaget's stages," then the evaluation of mastery of that objective simply becomes a short answer question (oral or written) in which the learner is asked to define and give an example of each stage.

Finally, objectives provide a useful means of communicating to administrators, other instructors, and community or professional groups the nature of what was included in the instruction. It can be useful for an instructor in the next course in the program to know what has been previously learned. Curriculum or evaluation committees may find such information valuable for planning. Professional associations or community groups may wish to confirm that the needs of learners are being met.

There are several commonly raised objections to the use of objectives. Instructors often argue that the development of objectives is time-consuming and actually takes away from more productive planning time. This feeling most often arises from a misperception of the amount of detail that is necessary. Obviously, if an instructor believes that ten or twenty objectives need to be written for each class, it becomes an overwhelming and counterproductive task. The actual degree of detail depends on the level of instruction and the subject area (teaching a skill to handicapped adults will, for example, require smaller and more detailed steps than teaching research skills to graduate social work students); however, the task should never become an overwhelming one. If it appears that objective writing is taking away from other planning activities, too much detail is probably being included.

A second commonly mentioned concern is that stating objectives will lead to a rigid instructional approach: once the objectives are written, there appears to be little room to incorporate unexpected learner interests or relevant current issues. Again, this issue tends to be one of balance. Objectives do not necessarily lead to an inflexible approach to instruction, although they can if the instructor feels unable to make changes as a session progresses and if no provision for flexible time has been made in the planning. It is usually the case, however, that student interests or current issues can be incorporated into previously stated objectives or added to a list of objectives.

Finally, instructors often believe that the use of objectives stifles creativity or independent thinking on the part of the learner. That is, if students are told exactly what to learn, the process becomes a matter of memorizing that information and regurgitating it on tests or in assignments. This concern is usually a consequence of a misunderstanding of the nature of objectives—a belief that they are only concerned with basic knowledge or rote learning and that the learner has no input into the objectives. Objectives can be developed that address high-level or creative thinking, and most adult learners should be involved in some way in the development of objectives.

In summary, objectives provide useful information to learners, assist instructors in the planning process, and are important in communicating with individuals or groups who need information about a course. It is often felt that objectives are too time-consuming, that they result in inflexible instruction or the "spoon-feeding" of students; however these objections are most often a result of false assumptions or a mis-use of objectives. To paraphrase a classic statement on writing objectives (Mager, 1962), we need to know where we're going before we can get there.

How to Write Objectives

The writing of objectives is a skill that requires practice and feedback from others. In some subject areas and at some levels of instruction, the process is easier simply because the nature of learning is more concrete or more observable. However, the sequence of steps given below can be applied to any area of instruction.

1. List, in any terms, the topics or goals of the instruction, using the degree of detail that seems appropriate to the learners. This list may include such items as: participants will learn to develop multiple choice tests; be able to write FORTRAN programs; appreciate the novels of Thomas Mann; or, be able to relate well to clients.

2. Translate items on the list into observable or measurable terms. This does not imply that any item should be made trivial; rather, ask what learner responses or behaviors adequately represent the original item. For example, appreciating the novels of Thomas Mann might imply that individuals could write a critique of one or more novel; relating well to clients could mean that clients make positive statements about the participants or that specific verbal or non-verbal communication skills are used.

3. For each statement that has been translated into observable behaviors or learner products, consider the degree of detail or specificity. Although this judgement is relative to the level of instruction and the characteristics of the audience, there may be statements which should be subdivided for clarity or combined for convenience. For remedial instruction or for lower levels, the steps will most likely be smaller, and consequently, the objectives more detailed. At higher levels, instruction may encompass broader concepts and syntheses of ideas, and the objectives will reflect this approach.

4. Consider, for each objective, any circumstances or conditions under which the learning will take place. For example, will the learners expect to solve problems with or without the use of calculators? Are there time constraints on performance? Is there room for error in the problem-solving process? If there are conditions of this nature for any objective, both learner and instructor will want to make these explicit at the outset. Where it is relevant, the objective should be rewritten to include this information.

5. Have the objective reviewed by one or more of the following individuals: colleagues teaching in the same subject area, individuals who have completed the course, or an instructional

design expert. Each of these categories of reviewers can provide slightly different information. However, the goal is to ensure that the objectives contain no ambiguous terms or vague descriptions of student behaviors or products. The purpose of objectives is the communication of the intended learning. If an objective fails to convey the goal of the instruction, then revision is called for. It is useful, in the review process, to ask specific questions of the reviewers. For example, colleagues might be asked to assess whether or not the objectives adequately reflect the content of the course; former participants might be asked whether or not these objectives identify skills that they obtained from the course; and instructional design experts could comment on whether or not the objectives contain measurable behaviors.

6. Finally, regardless of the degree of learner input into the development of the objectives, discuss the objectives with the learners and be prepared to revise them if they are not clear or comprehensive. As will be discussed in Chapter Seven, on-going evaluation is a valuable component of instructional planning. If the learners do not feel that the objectives are clear or that they adequately represent their interests or needs, make revisions.

The process of writing objectives is usually an iterative one; that is, general goals or statements of expectations are first listed, then translated into more specific behaviors. Comments from colleagues and learners lead to further revision, and finally the first try-out may reveal that additional changes are called for.

Types of Objectives

Every educator is aware that there are different types of learning. Expected learning can range from the simple rote learning of facts, terms, and definitions to the complex skills required in producing a research paper. In addition, some subject areas emphasize physical performance or the development of value systems. Different types of learning require different teaching and evaluation techniques. It is essential, therefore, that the type of learning be specified early in the planning process.

Although it is recognized that distinctions among types of learning may not be clear at all times, the commonly used organizational structure will be presented.

Domains of Learning

Learning can be separated into three domains or general areas. The first and largest area has been labelled the *cognitive domain*. This type of learning includes all intellectual processes: the recall of definitions, terms, names, and dates; the comprehension of concepts; the application of principles or formulae to the solution of problems; the analysis of ideas presented by others. Generally, the cognitive domain contains all that we traditionally think of as learning and encompasses most of what is usually described as being part of education. It is, however, only one aspect of learning. The second area is called the *affective domain* and includes values, attitudes, beliefs, emotions, motivation, and interests. In most situations, there is, at least, the implicit objective that participants will be interested in the subject area or that they will be motivated to learn. In other areas, such as the professions of nursing or social work or medicine, the values and attitudes of learners are an integral part of the training and should often be contained in explicitly stated objectives. In the arts, "enjoyment" and "appreciation" contain a large affective component. Overall, the affective domain includes emotional responses rather than intellectual ones, and as such, it may be difficult to describe in the previously defined objective format; however, it is often a major component of instructional goals. The third area of learning is the *psychomotor domain*, including any physical performance. In disciplines such as physical education, this description is clear: individuals learning tennis, for example, are mastering a set of physical skills. However, the psychomotor domain is relevant in many areas such as crafts, dance, second language learning (the physical production of sounds), medicine, and nursing. This type of learning includes the finely coordinated movements that are a part of technical skills (filling a tooth, using a lathe, drawing) as well as non-verbal communication or portraying feelings through body movements (drama, the learning of interpersonal skill in psychiatry or social work).

As can be seen from these brief descriptions, there will be many instructional situations in which the learning domains overlap or are difficult to separate. In the affective and psychomotor areas, in particular, there is usually a cognitive component as well. In the learning of a technical skill, one must first "know" the steps to be performed, in a cognitive sense, then practice the physical skill. Affective objectives involving the development of value systems also include the cognitive knowledge on which those values are based.

Levels of Learning

Although recognizing the domains of learning is useful in itself for planning instruction, there is a wide variety of types of learning within each domain. Again, these types or levels of learning can be extremely important for the selection of teaching methods, materials, and evaluation techniques. To take an example from the cognitive domain, participants learning to recognize varieties of trees would be involved in a quite different instructional situation from those who were developing a woodlot management plan. The most commonly used taxonomies of learning will be presented for each of the three domains; alternatives are also available and will be listed in the references at the end of the chapter.

Cognitive Domain

Bloom (1956) developed a six-level taxonomy for the cognitive domain. This taxonomy is intended to be hierarchical; that is, learning is facilitated by dealing with the content at the lower levels before exposure to materials at a higher level. This point will be illustrated further as the levels are presented.

The lowest level (the simplest type of learning) is called *knowledge*. This level includes the recognition and recall of basic facts and can be thought of as rote learning. Examples are:

1. The learner will be able to label the parts of the ear when a drawing is provided.

2. The learner will be able to define each of the three domains of learning in an instructional design model.

3. The learner will be able to recognize ten varieties of flowers when given sketches of flowers.

This level does not imply any understanding of the content, only the recognition or reproduction of material.

The second level of learning, moving up the hierarchy, is called *comprehension*. At this stage, objectives are stated in terms of understanding of the content: The learner not only "knows" the content but can demonstrate comprehension of it. Example objectives are:

1. The learner will be able to illustrate each of the three domains of learning with examples from his own subject area.

2. The learner will be able to describe in his own words behaviors associated with autism.

3. The learner will be able to explain the procedure for performing a binary search for a name in a telephone directory.

It is sometimes difficult to be sure that objectives at this level actually do involve comprehension and not rote knowledge. Criteria that assist in this distinction are the use of unique wording, elaboration of a definition or concept, and the providing of illustration or examples.

The third level in the taxonomy has been labelled *application*. As the name implies, this type of learning involves the use of rules, principles, or other basic knowledge in the solving of problems or in any new context. It is, literally, the application of previously learned knowledge in any new situations. Examples of objectives at the application level are:

1. The learner will be able to use the t-test formula to determine whether or not the means of two sets of data are significantly different from each other.

2. The learner will be able to write an objective in the affective domain of learning.

3. The learner will be able to correctly multiply 8 out of 10 pairs of two-digit numbers.

The application level is one of the easier areas in which objectives can be written; the products of application are usually clear and observable (e.g. correct solutions to problems).

Analysis is the fourth level in the hierarchy. At this stage, learners are able to "take apart" the component parts of a content area and to understand the relationships among ideas. The ability to compare and contrast is also a part of this level of learning. Examples are:

1. Given a short story by John Updike with which the learner is not familiar, she will be able to identify and describe the five stages of the short story structure, indicating any elements which are not present.

2. The learner will be able to explain three major differences between the theories of Freud and Jung.

3. While observing a squash match, the learner will be able to compare and contrast the strategies used by the two players.

As can be seen by the examples and the description of the analysis stage, this type of learning is more complex than the previous levels and is dependent on the understanding of the various components of the subject area being analyzed. It can be argued in some cases that the application level is not a necessary prerequisite for analysis; however, this varies with the discipline.

The next level in Bloom's taxonomy is *synthesis*. This type of learning includes a wide array of complex activities and, as the label implies, involves the putting together of information, concepts, or positions from a variety of sources into one product. The writing of an essay or term paper, the production of a computer program, or the formulation of a proposal or plan require the synthesis of ideas. At the more advanced levels of instruction in any area, synthesis will be a common expectation. Some examples are:

1. The learner will be able to write a research proposal which includes a research question, brief review of the literature, and a suggested methodology for answering the question.

2. The learner will develop and implement a computer program which simulates freeway traffic on the Trans-Canada Decarie interchange during rush hour.

3. The learner will prepare a paper to be given to the class on the effect of the defeat of the Equal Rights Amendment on the status of women.

Although obviously more difficult to evaluate and teach, the synthesis level of learning is often one of the major goals in instruction.

The highest level is *evaluation*. This stage includes judgements of quality based on criteria. The learner reads a novel or a research article or observes a performance and determines whether or not those products meet certain criteria. It is not an emotional response, but rather an objective evaluation based on a cognitive knowledge of what should be involved in some piece of work. Examples of evaluation are:

1. After reading a research article, the learner will be able to write a critique which describes any methodological flaws and also the strengths of the research.

2. The learner will be able to evaluate the strengths and limitations of this instructional design book, including as a basis of comparison, the evaluation of one other textbook with a similar purpose.

3. After observing a figure skating competition, the learner will be able to rank each participant on the basis of technical skill, style, and creativity.

The evaluation level of learning is most often relevant in the more advanced stages of instruction. This is not to say that evaluation-level objectives are inappropriate in new situations, but rather that a comprehensive knowledge of the subject area must be the basis for evaluative learning.

In summary, Bloom's taxonomy provides a mechanism for the organization of types of learning within the cognitive domain. Although the discrimination among these levels may seem somewhat arbitrary at times, it should be clear that the classification of objectives is valuable in instructional planning. The sequence of instruction can depend on the complexity of the learning (e.g. knowledge is necessary before application can occur). Teaching methods and materials must vary based on the level of learning, and obviously, more complex learning is evaluated using different techniques than those used for simpler learning.

Affective Domain

In the affective domain, the hierarchical aspect of learning is less clear. However a taxonomy has been developed which is useful in the organization of types of learning. Krathwohl, Bloom, and Masia (1964) describe five levels of learning in the affective domain.

The lowest level is called *receiving*, and at this stage, the learner simply attends to information, is aware of and willing to receive a value, belief, or attitude. This behavior may include observing or listening to attitudes expressed on an issue, an art exhibit, or a particular selection of music. As in the lowest level of the cognitive domain, no comprehension is implied; simply the learner willingly receives the information. Examples of objectives at the receiving level of the affective domain are:

1. The learner will participate in a walking tour of Old Montreal in order to observe architectural styles.

2. The learner will listen to Tchaikovsky's Piano Concerto No. 1.

3. The learner will read two poems by Sylvia Plath.

At this level, the individual does not respond in any way to the phenomena presented. It is only expected that attention be paid or that the information is received.

The second level of the affective domain, *responding*, involves "active" attending to the presentation of values, opinions, beliefs, etc. That is, the learner responds to the information presented in either a positive or negative manner. In addition to listening to a talk on human rights, the learner will be able to express some opinion on the issue. Examples of objectives could include:

1. After a tennis lesson, the participant will voluntarily make a statement concerning enjoyment of the game.

2. The learner will express an interest in taking a further course in instructional design.

3. The learner will voluntarily participate in a discussion on the issue of abortion.

As illustrated by the above examples, this level of the affective domain contains the expression of interest, enjoyment, opinion, or attitudes. At this point the individual does not demonstrate a commitment to the response.

Valuing is the third level of the affective domain. At this stage, the learner shows consistency and commitment to beliefs, values, and attitudes. It is clear that a value is preferred and acted upon. There are not, as yet, established ideas as to the interrelationships among values or beliefs; however, values or beliefs have been accepted and form the foundation for behaviors. Examples are:

1. After the completion of a course in downhill skiing, the learner voluntarily purchases lift tickets and skis at least one day per week.

2. During a course in women's studies, the learner organizes or voluntarily participates in an anti-pornography demonstration.

3. Following a discussion of Margaret Atwood's early novel, *Surfacing*, the learner reads at least two other novels by the same author.

This level of affective learning is usually the minimum that we wish our audience to achieve. That is, we hope that individuals will demonstrate a consistency of affective responses and will act based on what they have learned.

In the fourth level, *organization*, learners organize values, beliefs, and attitudes into a system, determine the interrelationships among them, and select the strongest ones. Rather than demonstrating commitment to isolated values (I believe in euthanasia), the individual demonstrates a more complex value system. Examples are:

1. The learner will read several authors' views of the ethics of social-worker/patient interactions and formulate a personal set of guidelines.

2. After reading at least ten novels by modern Canadian writers, the learner will be able to describe which aspects of the writing are preferred and compare the novels on that basis.

3. The learner will write an article for the local newspaper on the issue of conservation of resources versus technological advancement.

The major difference between the organization level and lower levels in the affective domain is the presence of several values, beliefs, or attitudes, and the exploration of the relationships between them.

The fifth and final level in the affective domain is *characterization* by a value, or alternatively, value complex. As the label implies, at this stage, the learner has adopted a belief or value system to such an extent that the individual is characterized by that value; for example: "She is a feminist"; "He is a communist." This level of learning can also be described as a philosophy of life or a world view. Example objectives could be:

1. The learner will become a professional musician.

2. The learner will be able to describe, in essay form, his philosophy of life.

3. Upon reading this book, the learner will change careers and become an instructional design consultant.

As can be seen from the examples given, objectives at this level are not commonly used; they are most relevant at very advanced stages of instruction, and usually, in the situations where they are appropriate, the learners have already reached a high level of commitment.

To summarize, the Krathwohl et al. (1964) taxonomy provides a useful organizational scheme for the affective domain. The use of the taxonomy encourages awareness of different levels of learning in this domain; we too often think of values or interests as existing or not existing, rather than as evolving through developmental stages. In subject areas where the affective domain is an integral component of the learning, the organization of instruction according to this taxonomy would be beneficial.

Psychomotor Domain

In the psychomotor domain, various organizational schemes have been developed by educators, some of which could be called hierarchical, and others which appear to be categorical, although they are presented as taxonomies. An example of a more categorical system (Kibler, Barker, & Miles 1970) includes the levels of gross body movements (running, jumping), finely coordinated body movements (driving a car, operating a lathe), non-verbal communication (mime, facial expression) and speech (pronunciation of sounds). If this system seems useful, the relevant article listed in the bibliography should be consulted. The taxonomy to be presented in this chapter (Simpson, 1966) more closely resembles those suggested for the cognitive and affective domains; that is, the objectives that are classified at the lower levels are simpler to master, and in general, the higher levels depend on the lower levels.

The first level, called *perception*, includes the awareness of objects in the environment through the senses and the association of those objects (or cues) with the task to be performed. Although this is not actually a physical activity in itself, it is seen to be the basis for all psychomotor learning in much the same way that receiving is the basis for affective learning. Example objectives are:

1. The learner will be able to discriminate among colours to be used in oil painting.

2. The learner will recognize the angle at which a squash ball bounces from the wall before swinging the racquet.

3. The learner will be able to distinguish, by touch, four different types of fabric.

If these basic perceptual skills are not present or learned, the psychomotor skills which are based on them cannot be mastered. It is often important, therefore, to check that the perceptual skills are present and if not, to include them in the instruction.

The second level, called *set*, is described as the preparatory adjustment or readiness for a particular kind of action. This may involve a mental set, as in knowing what the steps of the performance will be; a physical set, where the body is in the appropriate stance or position; or an emotional set, which is a willingness or desire to perform. Examples are:

1. The learner will be able to list the steps required in preparing a soufflé.

2. The learner will be able to position himself to receive a tennis serve.

3. The learner will state an interest in improving his ability to operate a sewing machine.

As with level one, this level is still at the beginning or basic stages of psychomotor learning but is essential for further achievement. Again, it is important to ensure that the audience has reached this step before continuing.

The third level of the psychomotor domain is called *guided response*. At this stage, individuals perform the specific skillful actions which will become the components of more complex tasks. Skillful actions are often imitated from a model or may be done by trial and error with adjustments being made based on feedback from the consequences of the performance. Examples are:

1. The learner will be able to follow the instructor's path in performing one parallel turn on downhill skis.

2. The learner will be able to maintain appropriate eye contact with a client by judging the client's responses.

3. The learner will be able to cook a white wine sauce by following a recipe.

This level of the psychomotor domain can be seen as the first step in developing a skill. The learner is discovering or replicating the first component parts of the task which will become habitual with practice.

At the fourth level, *mechanism*, the behaviors learned with guidance or modelling become habitual, and the learner is proficient at carrying them out. For example:

1. The learner will be able independently to use the herringbone step to ascend a hill on cross country skis.

2. The learner will be able to administer an intravenous needle.

3. The learner will be able to sand a piece of wood to a prespecified degree of fineness.

This level of psychomotor learning usually represents the degree of achievement desired; the learner expects independently and proficiently to execute a specific task.

The next level is called the *complex overt response*. Here, learners are involved in more complex tasks, involving complex patterns or sequences of movements, and the actions are performed without hesitation, or automatically. Examples are:

1. The learner will be able to perform the basic steps of a western square dance.

2. The learner will be able to prepare and serve a three-course dinner.

3. The learner will be able to operate a mill machine.

As illustrated by the examples given above, at this stage the individual can perform tasks efficiently which involve a set of component skills, these skills usually being structured in a pattern or sequence of movements or activities.

The sixth level, *adaptation*, occurs when learners are able to adapt motor activities to meet unanticipated demands of the situation. In most sports (baseball, tennis), the individual must respond quickly to moves made by the opponent or other members of the team. In interpersonal situations, non-verbal communication will depend on other individuals in the interaction. Examples are:

1. The learner will be able to play a game of golf.

2. The learner will be able to conduct a preliminary physical check-up on a patient.

3. The learner will be able to train a dog to sit, stay, and retrieve.

At this more advanced level of the psychomotor domain, the learner is able to choose movements or skills to be used, based on the immediately preceding action. This clearly requires a well-developed repertoire of skills and the knowledge of when each is appropriate.

The final, seventh level of learning is *origination*, the ability to create new motor actions based on previously developed skills. For example:

1. The learner will be able to create a modern dance routine based on previously learned steps and sub-routines.

2. The learner will originate a series of drills for the practice of forehand and backhand swings in squash.

3. The learner will demonstrate a unique technique for communicating with a deaf child.

This level of psychomotor learning parallels the highest levels of the cognitive and affective domains. That is, the audience has completely mastered the component parts of a skill and is now able to originate and create, using previously learned abilities.

In summary, the use of a taxonomy in the psychomotor domain serves the same purpose as it does in the cognitive and affective domains. The awareness of the stages of learning a particular skill is important in ensuring that instruction includes the necessary prerequisite behaviors.

Objectives and the Adult Learner

Various characteristics of the adult learner have been discussed which have an influence on the way in which objectives are used in instruction. The adult is usually self-directed or moving toward self-direction; the adult prefers to have input into or responsibility for what he learns; the adult benefits from instruction that is related to his past experience; the adult most often has immediate, concrete learning goals. When these characteristics are present, it clearly is not appropriate to preplan a set of objectives, hand them out to your audience, and carry on with the agenda. However, it *is* essential that everyone in the situation, instructor and audience, know where the instruction is going, and stated objectives are the most efficient way of communicating this intent. The following guidelines suggest techniques for using objectives with the adult learner.

1. Collect as much information as possible about your audience before beginning the planning of the instruction. This process is called "needs assessment" and can be conducted in a comprehensive and formal way or fairly informally, depending on the situation you are in. If, for example, you are offering an in-service workshop, you could include a questionnaire with the registration forms, asking participants to indicate their previous experience with the topic, their interests in the topic, their needs, or any other information you feel will be useful. If you are offering a course in a structured program, information about the audience is often available from records or from other instructors in the same program. In a general interest course or a continuing education course, the first session can be dedicated to a discussion of participants' interests, background, needs, and experience. Other times, the very fact that participants have chosen to attend the session will provide you with the necessary, basic information: for example, a session on the use of insecticides in grape growing will be attended by individuals who are growing grapes or planning to grow grapes and who need this information for their work. Regardless of the way the information is collected, objectives should always be developed with the characteristics of the audience in mind.

2. When you first meet your audience, there should be some opportunity for them to have input into the objectives you have developed. In a course, this can be done in the first session; even in a two-hour workshop, the first 20 minutes can and should be dedicated to a discussion of the appropriateness of the objectives for that audience. The strategy that is used to obtain this input will determine the amount of input. If, for example, a set of prepared objectives are handed out at the beginning of a session and the participants are asked to read them over and make suggestions for changes, additions, or deletions, the amount of change will be relatively small. Most learners, in a new situation, are reluctant to make major changes in a prepared agenda. However, depending on your audience, this may be the most appropriate strategy. Individuals who are new to a subject area, anxious or uncomfortable, lacking in confidence, etc., are not likely to *want* to initiate many changes; asking them to do so will only increase the discomfort or anxiety. With a more independent, mature, experienced, or confident audience, input into the objectives should be asked for *before* handing out any prepared list. The session can begin with a general discussion of the parameters of the course, workshop, or meeting, then move into what the audience expects to get out of the session. Most often, if you have collected adequate information about the audience in advance, the expectations will match the planned objectives to a large extent, and they can be modified on the spot.

3. When working with an audience which has extensive experience or background in the area, the objectives can be written collaboratively with the learners. This is not practical for a one-time workshop or any session that is shorter than one day, but is very effective for longer segments of instruction. Participants might work in groups to generate topics of interest in the area, presenting the results of their work to the larger group. Discussion among all participants can then lead to a list of topics or activities which subsequently can be translated into objectives.

4. Finally, with an experienced, independent audience which also has a set of diverse interests or needs, objectives can be negotiated individually between the instructor and each learner, leading to contracts for grading purposes (if required) or to less

formal agreements as to what activities or projects will be worked on. The instructor then assumes a role of resource person, facilitator, and manager.

Seeming contradictions between the use of objectives and the principles of adult education are resolved when one thinks of the learner as a contributor to the design of the instruction. The degree of contribution is determined by the degree of maturity, experience, or independence of the learner. Not all adults are ready or able or willing to develop their own objectives, but every adult learner should have some opportunity to say what they expect from the situation.

CHAPTER FOUR
SEQUENCING INSTRUCTION

The sequencing of instruction—determining the order in which topics or objectives will be taught—is frequently overlooked in the planning stages, or it may simply be dictated by some convenient guideline. Often, the order of chapters in a textbook, the order in which the instructor learned the material, or the chronological or historical order will determine the ordering of course topics. We often know intuitively, however, that many skills and more complex types of learning cannot be mastered without the more basic underlying skills or knowledge already being part of the learner's repertoire. One cannot, for example, master the statistical concept of regression without a comprehension of correlation, or play a game of racquet ball without having developed the eye-hand coordination necessary to hit the ball, or state a preference for Bach without having heard any of his compositions. In these examples (one from each of the three domains of learning), it will be noted that the necessary underlying skill or knowledge, the prerequisite, is from a lower level in the taxonomy. In fact, as was discussed in Chapter Three, the taxonomies in each domain were developed so as to be hierarchical: the lower-level, simpler types of learning must be prerequisites to the higher-level, more complex types of learning. Although some subject areas lend themselves more readily to this type of structure than others, the taxonomies can often provide a useful guide as to what objectives should precede or follow others in the instructional sequences.

It is not necessarily the case, though, that a comprehension level objective must always be learned before an application level objective; this decision is based on whether the learning of the content of the latter is dependent on mastery of the lower-level objective. (Must an individual know this in order to be able to learn that?) The process of determining which learning must precede which other learning is called *instructional analysis*. The reader should be warned, at this point, that several different terms are used in the literature to refer to analysis techniques. Here instructional analysis will be used to refer to any systematic procedure for analyzing the content of a course or a segment of a course in order to plan the sequence of the instruction. Two common techniques will be defined and described in the following section.

The advantages to conducting an instructional analysis are fairly clear. First, in some subject areas, learners literally cannot master an objective in the absence of the prerequisite knowledge or skills. Without an analysis of the content, the instructor, who is usually an experienced subject expert, may not be aware of those prerequisites and thus may experience a frustrating teaching and learning experience. Second, the completion of an instructional analysis often leads the instructor to assess "entering" or pre-instruction skills, which provides valuable information for both teacher and learner. The appropriateness of the level of instruction can be judged and revised if necessary. Third, experienced adult learners can be given a copy of an instructional analysis and, with some assistance, can use it as a self-assessment and study guide. Productive use of the analysis depends, of course, on frequent reference to it during the instruction. Fourth, a comprehensive analysis of course content leads the instructor to an awareness of the levels of learning included in the course. It is often with surprise that an instructor discovers that the majority of the objectives are at the knowledge or comprehension level of learning when the intention was to teach the higher levels of synthesis or evaluation. Finally, instructional analysis can assist in the evaluation of learning. If the subject area is organized in a hierarchical structure, then mastery of the higher-level objectives indicates that the prerequisites are also mastered.

There are, on the other hand, some commonly raised objections to instructional analysis. First, and understandably, it is often stated that instructional analysis is far too time-consuming and complex. When this is clearly the case, the compromise position might be to conduct analyses only for a segment of the content that is particularly difficult to teach or learn. Also, it should be pointed out that in some subject areas the types of analyses being discussed here may not be appropriate. Some alternatives will be presented later in the chapter. Second, it is sometimes felt that an analysis of the instructional content imposes too much structure on the teaching process, detracts from spontaneity, and reduces the instructor to a version of a teaching machine. As with any other component of instructional planning, the plan should always remain flexible and be revised if feedback indicates that anyone is bored, confused, or not learning. The only visible effect of using an instructional analysis should be increased efficiency in teaching and learning. If the process begins to detract from the content, the technique is not being properly utilized.

A systematic, structured approach to instruction may appear to contradict many of the principles of adult learning. However, planning only facilitates learning; the degree to which the learner participates in that planning depends on the characteristics of the audience. The mature, experienced, self-directed adult learner could work with a group of peers or with the instructor to conduct an instructional analysis of the area under study. The more dependent adult or the adult in a new learning situation usually prefers to rely on the instructor for the sequencing of the content; as experience is gained more contributions can be made to the planning process.

To summarize briefly, instructional analysis is simply a systematic procedure for sequencing instruction in order to optimize learning. In many subject areas, individuals simply must master some objectives before beginning to learn others; in other areas, this hierarchical structure is not as apparent. However some organization of the content will make both teaching and learning easier.

Types of Instructional Analyses

Two commonly used types of instructional analysis will be described, and in the following section, a step-by-step procedure will be given for each type. Finally, some alternative sequencing principles will be discussed. It is advisable, however, to read through and consider the two instructional analyses, even though the immediate applicability may not be obvious.

Task Analysis

Based on the assumption that learning is hierarchical in nature, task analysis is the procedure for determining which specific aspects of learning must precede others in order that mastery of an objective or goal can take place. Gagné (1975) originally described task analysis in terms of his own hierarchy of cognitive skills; however, the procedure is now commonly used with reference to the taxonomies of learning described in Chapter Three. The steps involved in conducting a task analysis, with examples, will be discussed shortly. At this point, it is important to realize that in task analysis one considers the steps that a learner must go through in mastering a skill or objective. It is this feature that distinguishes this instructional sequence from others to be presented.

Procedural Analysis

Procedural analysis emphasizes the actual order in which a learner performs a task, as opposed to the hierarchy of skills involved. As such, it is often used for the psychomotor domain, or in situations where there is little variation in the levels of learning. For those readers who are familiar with the technique of developing flow charts, a procedural analysis is an equivalent process. In teaching a handicapped adult to dial a telephone, for example, the procedural analysis would indicate that first the receiver should be lifted from the hook, the learner should then listen for a dial tone, if a dial tone was heard, the next step should be performed, and so on. The analysis consists of the breakdown of a task into steps that must be performed, in the order in which they are actually performed. This is quite different from the examination of the hierarchical nature of the learning process, as is done in task analysis. In general terms, it is an analysis of the order in which components of a task are performed, versus an analysis of the order in which components of a task must be learned.

How to Conduct Instructional Analysis

Task Analysis

The procedure for doing a task analysis will be given, then illustrated with examples. The procedure is an elaborated and slightly modified form of that suggested by Gagné (1975).

1. Select the objectives upon which the analysis will be performed. This may include the one final or overall objective of the course, a few high-level, complex objectives, or in some cases, the majority of the objectives in a course. This decision depends primarily on the level of the learners and possibly on the subject area. In an introductory course in sociology, for example, there may be four main objectives, each of about equal importance, which should be analyzed. In teaching mathematics in an academic upgrading class, it is probably valuable to analyze the majority of the objectives. In general, if individuals are learning in smaller steps and if they have fewer prerequisites, more detailed analyses will be useful.

2. Considering one objective at a time, ask yourself, "What must the person know in order to begin to learn this objective?" If necessary, make a list of these prerequisites, not considering any particular order at this point.

3. For each of the items listed in step 2, again ask yourself, "What must the person know in order to begin to learn this?" Again, make lists if necessary.

4. Repeat this process until you feel that you have reached the likely pre-instruction level of the audience. This is often a difficult decision, and a commonly asked question is, "How far back should I go?" If you have previous experience with the content or if you can obtain information from colleagues as to the usual entering level of the audience, use that as a guideline. Otherwise, carry the task analysis to a slightly lower level than you might expect of the learners and be prepared to revise it.

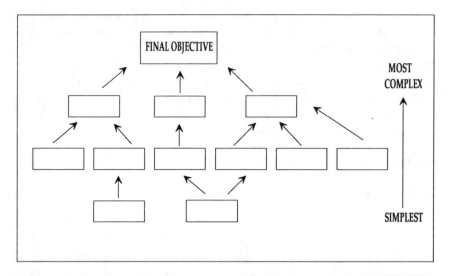

Figure 4-1. Each arrow indicates that the learning below is a necessary prerequisite for the learning above.

5. Go back to the lists that you have made at each level of steps 3 and 4 and arrange each item in a "tree structure":

6. Ask an experienced learner or a colleague who is a subject area expert to review your analysis. Explain the structure of the analysis and ask your reviewer to look for both gaps and relationships between items that are not valid. Revise if necessary.

7. Use the analysis in your instruction. You will be able to validate it by observing where individuals experience difficulty or confusion. Also, in the try-out stage, assess the learning at each level of the analysis. If there are instances where your audience mastered a higher-level objective but not the lower-level objective, this will indicate a flaw in your analysis.

Example One.

This procedure will be first illustrated using the content of Chapter Three. The course is one in instructional design and is a required course for people obtaining a diploma in college teaching. The audience has a wide variety of backgrounds, both in subject area and amount of teaching experience.

1. Although task analyses would likely be performed on several objectives, for this course, the one chosen for this illustration will be:

"The learners will be able to write a set of objectives for a course in their own subject area."

This is a high-level objective, the synthesis level in the cognitive domain, and although it is quite general, this is probably appropriate for the audience.

2. The second step involves asking the question, "What must the person know in order to begin to learn this objective?" This list should be given in sentences or phrases which are close to being objectives in themselves; it will be necessary at a later stage to be able to evaluate learners' mastery of the components of the task analysis. The list then, may contain: the learner should, before beginning to learn this objective, be able to:

a) define "objective"

b) recognize a well-stated objective

c) distinguish between vague and observable words or phrases

d) state the degree of detail or specificity required in the particular course

e) describe situations in which any special conditions should be made explicit.

As can be seen, this list is not yet in any particular order, and it may not, in fact, be complete. However, it is a first attempt at describing the components of the content.

3. In the third step, each of the items in the previous list is examined, and the same question is asked, "What must the person know in order to begin to learn this?" Going back to the second step:

a) define "objective"
   • no previous knowledge required

b) recognize a well-stated objective.
   The learner should be able to:
   • define "objective"
   • list the criteria of a well-stated objective.

c) distinguish between vague and observable words or phrases.
   The learner should be able to:
   • recognize vague or unobservable words or phrases
   • recognize observable words or phrases.

d) state the degree of detail or specificity required in the particular course.
   The learner should be able to:
   • describe the level of competence of the class in the subject area.

e) describe situations in which any special conditions should be made explicit.
   The learner should be able to:

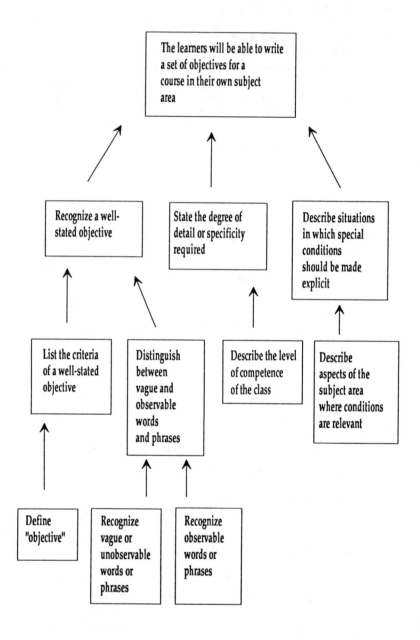

Figure 4–2: Preliminary Task Analysis for Example 1

- describe any aspects of the subject area where equipment, supplemental material, time, etc., are relevant.

4. In the fourth step, each of the components listed under step 3 is examined, and the same question is asked, "What must the person know in order to begin to learn this?" In this example, a review of the items in step 3 shows that the statements are all at the level at which the individual is likely to be entering the course. It is decided, therefore, that no further breakdown is required.

5. Based on the lists from the previous steps, an attempt is now made to organize the components into a hierarchical structure. The first analysis might yield the diagram in Figure 4-2.

6. Usually, at this point, the analysis is too familiar to allow the perception of flaws, and it becomes important to review it with colleagues or learners. In this example, it is quite likely that a reviewer would comment on the following:

- the learner should be able to *write a good objective* before writing a set of objectives
- the learner should be able to *generate* observable words or phrases (not merely recognize them) before writing objectives.

The task analysis would then be revised on the basis of the comments, possibly yielding the analysis given in figure 4-3. At this point, it should be emphasized that there is rarely *one* right task analysis; the structure often depends on the sophistication of the audience or the instructor's preferred structure or organization. In this example, it can probably now be assumed that no major gaps or illogical sequences still exist.

7. The final developmental step involves trying out the task analysis. Learning would take place starting at the bottom of the diagram and moving upwards. Areas where the learners encountered unexpected difficulty could be areas where the analysis was at fault. Also learning of any one of the components should imply mastery of the prerequisite components; if this does not occur, the analysis should be reexamined.

Example 2

The next example will utilize a more technical and complex subject structure. It is based on a consultation with an instructor of a computer science course, "Introduction to Data Structures." Although the content of the analysis may not be relevant or even comprehensible to many readers, it is valuable to follow the procedure once more. The class consisted of approximately 100 students in their third and fourth years of an undergraduate degree. Students had a variety of backgrounds in computer science, management, and engineering.

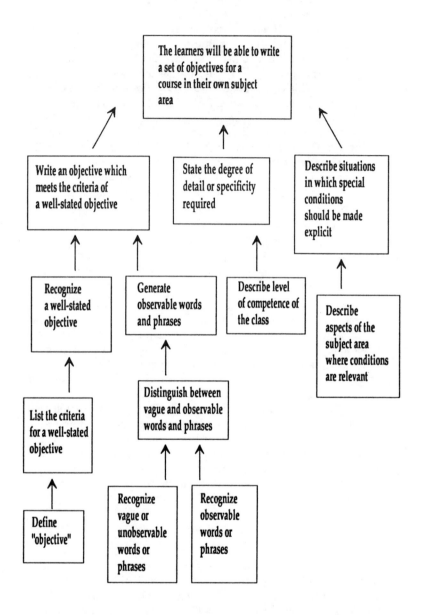

Figure 4–3: Revised Task Analysis for Example 1

1. In the first step, the objective that was chosen for analysis was:

"The student will be able to write a set of modular subroutines to operate on an object."

Although task analysis was not regularly performed in this course, this objective was chosen as one that was particularly difficult to teach, and one in which sequence or organization might be of particular importance.

2. In the second step, the instructor was asked, "What must the student know in order to begin to learn this objective?" He was able to supply the following analysis:

The student should be able to:

a) determine what operations are necessary

b) describe the use to which the object will be put

c) justify a choice for the implementation of the object

d) choose a suitable programming language

e) be able to write programs in a suitable language.

3. After the first analysis, step 3 involves, as in the previous example, going back to each of the components listed in step 2, and asking, "What must the student know in order to begin to learn this objective?" The result of this analysis yielded the following additions:

2(a) determine what operations are necessary

2(a1) describe the use to which the object will be put

2(b) describe the use to which the object will be put
  - entry behavior

2(c) justify the choice for the implementation of the object

2(c1) determine for a variety of implementations the "cost" of the operations

2(c2) Analyze an operation for a given implementation

2(c3) describe all possible implementations of the object

2(c4) compare two different implementations

2(c5) determine the criteria for evaluation of an implementation

2(d) choose a suitable programming language

2(d1) describe available languages and the features of those languages

2(d2) describe the efficiency of the available languages

2(e) write programs in a suitable language
  - entry behavior.

Aside from the process of continuing to determine what are the prerequisites of each component, it is important to note that at this step, some of the hierarchical arrangements might be revealed; that is 2(d) has become a prerequisite for 2(a) and 2(b) has no further breakdown.

4. In step 4, the same process is repeated, examining the components of step 3:

2(a1) describe the use to which the object will be put
- entry behavior

2(c1) determine for a variety of implementations the "cost" of the operations
- 2(c2) and 2(c3) are prerequisite learning

2(c2) analyze an operation for a given implementation
- the student should be able to perform a worst case analysis of an operation on an implementation

2(c3) compare all possible implementations of the object
- entry behavior

2(c3) compare two different implementations
- may be redundant

2(c5) determine the criteria for evaluation of an implementation
- may be redundant

Once more, the further analyses revealed that some components were subsets of others, for example 2(c2) and 2(c3) were prerequisite to 2(c1); also it became apparent that some behaviors had already been subsumed or included by others, e.g. 2(c4) and 2(c5) and thus were irrelevant.

5. In step 5 the first attempt is made to order these components into a hierarchical structure, based on the lists from the previous steps. This preliminary result is depicted in Figure 4-4.

6. In step 6, a reviewer commented on the following problems:

- the two components, "Determine what operations are necessary" and "Describe the use to which an object will be put" are actually prerequisites of "Describe all possible implementations of the object" and therefore should be replaced in the analysis.
- "Justify a choice for the implementation of the object" should include "making the choice"
- In the component, "Perform a worst case analysis of an operation in an implementation," it is really only necessary that the student be able to perform a worst case analysis, and therefore the condition should be deleted.

Revisions based on the review yielded the analysis in Figure 4-5.

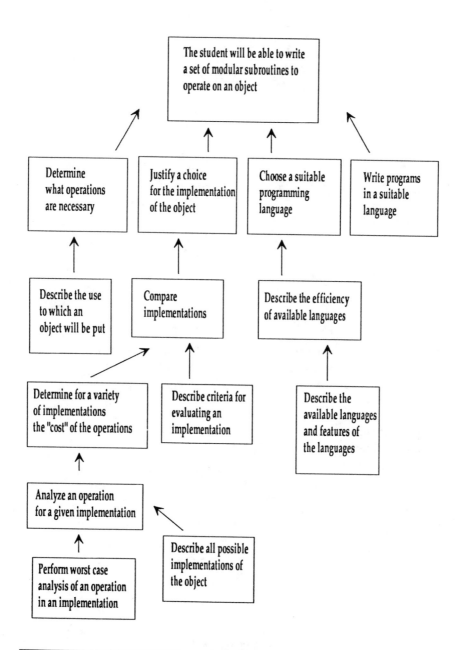

Figure 4–4: Preliminary Task Analysis for Example 2

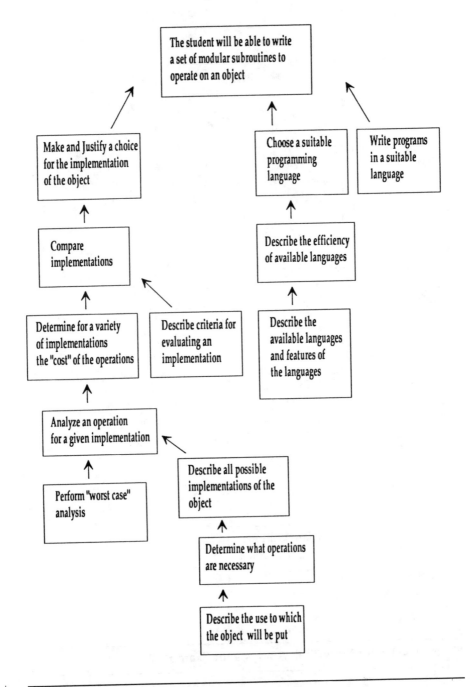

Figure 4–5: Revised Task Analysis for Example 2

7. As in the previous example, the next step involves trying out the task analysis in the teaching situations and making revisions based on students' learning.

Example 3.

One of the most common objections to the use of task analysis is that it is not appropriate in many subject areas, and particularly that it is never relevant to the affective domain. Although the procedure is admittedly much more difficult, it is often the case that instructors facing the formidable task of organizing high-level affective objectives do find that task analysis is a valuable technique. This third example is taken from the clinical teaching objectives of a college-level nursing program.

1. The specific objective chosen for analysis in step 1 was:

"The learner will be able to demonstrate caring behaviors in patient interaction in the clinical area."

One of many interpersonal objectives in the curriculum, this example was seen to be at a high level (value complex) in the affective domain, and also a difficult concept to "teach." As was pointed out in Chapter Three, the domains do tend to overlap, and it was expected by the nursing instructors that this objective would also contain cognitive and psychomotor components.

2. Next, the instructors responded to the question, "What must the individual know in order to begin to learn this objective?" The following answer was given:

The learner must be able to:

    a) identify caring behaviors in the clinical setting

    b) identify caring behaviors in the laboratory setting

    c) demonstrate caring behaviors in a role-playing situation with a classmate

    d) describe the essential behaviors of the caring relationship.

Although at this point the instructors did not feel that the list was adequate (the "value" component seemed to be missing), it was decided to continue with the process.

3. We returned to the first analysis in step 2 and again asked, for each item, "What must the individual know in order to begin to learn this objective?" Results were:

    2(a) identify caring behaviors in the clinical setting

    2(a1) define the concept of caring

    2(a2) list the characteristics of caring behavior (attentiveness, honesty, warmth, responsibility, etc.)

    2(b) identify caring behaviors in the laboratory setting

      • prerequisite learning is the same as for 2(a)

    2(c) demonstrate caring behaviors in a role-playing situation with a classmate

2*(c1)* identify caring behaviors in both clinical and laboratory settings

2*(d)* describe the essential behaviors of the caring relationship
  • prerequisite learning is the same as for 2(a).

As in the previous example, some of the items on the list from step 2 appeared to be dependent on each other.

4. The repeat analysis called for in step 4 revealed no further components.

5. Next, the first attempt to diagram the relationships was done. The result is given in Figure 4-6.

6. Since a group of instructors were involved in the analysis of this objective, the review process consisted of discussion among the instructors and with the instructional design consultant. The following concerns were raised, the major one being related to the issue raised under step 2, namely, that an important component had been overlooked.

The comments were:
  • the majority of the components in the analysis are cognitive, with only the final two being affective.
  • a gap exists between the cognitive and affective components, between moving from "describe" and "identify" to "demonstrate."
  • the separation between "identifying caring behaviors" in the clinical and the laboratory settings is artificial and should be eliminated.
  • if the clinical/laboratory distinction is eliminated, the analysis is left with only a linear progression, and this does not seem reasonable considering the complexity of the learning.

As can be seen, the nature of the reviewers' comments is quite different in this example: the criticisms are much more general, making revisions more difficult. This situation often will be encountered in the affective domain, reflecting the difficulty with which affective learning can be translated into objectives and organized comprehensively into a hierarchical sequence.

7. Again, the analysis will be tested in the teaching situation.

Evaluation of the learning in the affective domain will utilize observation techniques, a topic to be discussed in Chapter Six.

Procedural Analysis

As described earlier, procedural analysis is used when the objective contains a series of components to be performed in a sequence. The result of performing one part of the task puts the learner in the position, or gives the learner the product, to perform the next step or part of the

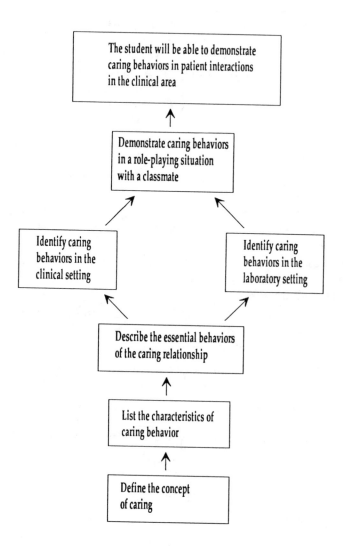

Figure 4–6: Preliminary Task Analysis for Example 3

task. Each of these parts could be taught independently; in other words, there is no hierarchy of learning, or required prerequisite learning.

A step-by-step guide for conducting a procedural analysis will be given, followed by examples.

1. Select the objectives for which procedural analysis seems appropriate. These objectives will most likely be in the psychomotor domain, or at least contain a large component of performance even though it may be based on previous cognitive or affective learning. The criterion for selecting objectives for procedural analysis is that they depend on a correct sequence of behaviors, each one of which could be taught separately.

2. For each objective, either visualize performing the task or actually perform it yourself, if possible. Record each step in the performance, in the sequence in which you performed them.

3. Return to your list of steps, consider (a) the "input" needed for the step; namely, the material, equipment, or previous performance required for the performance, (b) the "process"; that is, what behavior is done at this step, and (c) the "output" or the result of the step. Each "output" should be the input of the next step. The purpose of this review is to check for any gaps or out-of-sequence steps. Revise, if necessary.

4. Observe another individual performing the task. Using your list of steps as a checklist, note any discrepancies between the performance and your list. Revise if necessary.

5. Arrange the list into a procedural analysis diagram as in Figure 4-7:

Figure 4-7

Where the sequence of steps depends on a decision or the product of a previous step, the resulting analysis may have the format of Figure 4-8.

6. Use of the analysis in an instructional situation may lead to further revisions. As with the task analysis approach, if people experience confusion in moving from one step to another, this may indicate a flaw in the analysis.

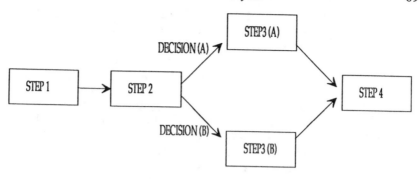

Example 1.

The situation chosen for the first example of procedural analysis was an intermediate level downhill skiing course for adults. The learners, at this stage of instruction, had all successfully completed a beginners' course in which they had mastered the prerequisite psychomotor skills. Therefore, at this time, objectives mainly involved executing previously learned skills in a particular sequence in order to perform more complex tasks. As such, the majority of the objectives in the course were suited for procedural rather than task analysis.

1. The objective chosen for this example was:

"The learner will be able to execute a parallel turn on downhill skis."

As mentioned above in the description of the course, mastery of this objective involves the sequential execution of skills that had been previously learned.

2. Visualizing the performance, the instructor listed the following steps:

The learner will

a) bend the knees maintaining body weight over the centre of the skis;

b) plant the ski pole, on the downhill side of the skis, about one foot away from the ski, just ahead of the front of the boot;

c) straighten the knees to standard skiing position, simultaneously unweighting the uphill ski and tilting both skis so that the downhill edges are biting into the surface while keeping both skis parallel;

d) as skis turn, return the pole to its standard position;

e) when turn is complete, return body weight to both skis;

3. In the third step, the instructor was asked to consider the input to, and the output from, each component listed in the previous step, in order to discover gaps or components that are not in sequence. This process yielded the following comments:

- the input to step 2(a) is not clear; it should be preceded by a description of the position immediately preceding the execution of the task.
- in step 2(c) several behaviors are dependent on each other, and there are several "inputs" and "outputs" involved; that is, straightening the knees yields the output that allows the unweighting of the uphill ski, even though they seem to occur simultaneously, and this then yields the position that allows the "edging."
- although step 2(d) follows the previous sequence, the wording may be misleading: the skis are allowed to turn "around the pole," and returning the pole to standard position signifies the completion of the turn (and the output for the next step).

Revisions based on this analysis yielded:

The learner will

3a) be in a position where skis are parallel, knees are slightly bent, and the body weight is centered over the skis;

b) bend the knees maintaining body weight over the centre of the skis;

c) plant the ski pole, on the downhill side of the ski, about one foot away from the ski, just ahead of the front of the boot;

d) straighten the knees to the standard skiing position;

e) unweight the uphill ski;

f) tilt both skis so that the downhill edges are biting into the surface;

g) allow the skis to turn the desired amount;

h) return the pole to its standard position;

i) return weight to both skis, as in the beginning position.

As can be seen, the procedure is now separated into smaller, or more unique components. Even though the initial visualizing process yielded several simultaneous behaviors, a consideration of input and output from each component revealed that these behaviors were in fact dependent on the occurrence of a previous behavior.

4. Observation of performance, in this example, yielded no further revisions. As with many quick-moving and complex tasks, it was found to be difficult to observe the separate behaviors. At times, a videotape of the performance will be of assistance when difficulties in the analysis are encountered.

5. The procedural analysis diagram is presented in Figure 4-9. During the diagramming process, step 3(g) became a decision behavior, rather than a step, since there was a judgment involved about the length of time that the previous step should be

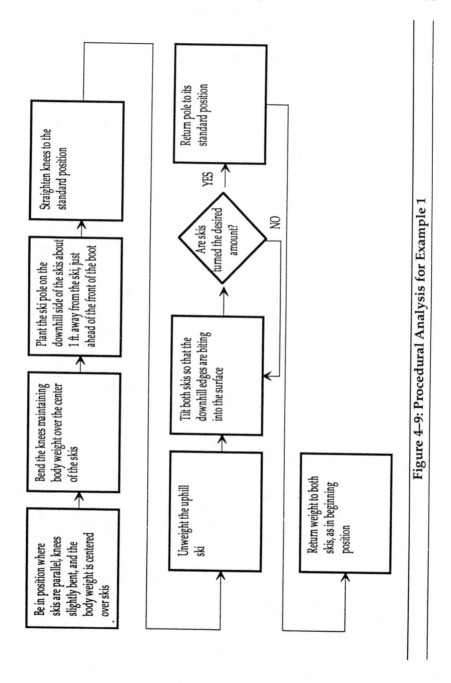

Figure 4–9: Procedural Analysis for Example 1

continued. Otherwise, this process was a simple translation from the revised list to the diagram.

6. Finally, the analysis is tested during instruction, and revisions are made when confusion appears or learning does not take place.

Example 2.

For this example, a college-level nursing instructor selected a task that is taught in the first year of a three-year program. Although the learning involved in this skill (preparing a needle for the injection of medication) is mainly in the psychomotor domain, the student must begin the task with several cognitive domain prerequisites. It may be useful in this case to use a combined task analysis and procedural analysis; however, for the purpose of this illustration, it will be assumed that the prerequisite objectives have been mastered.

1. The instructor gave the objective as:

"The student will be able to select the appropriate equipment, assemble the equipment, calculate and withdraw the appropriate dose of the medication Gravol."

This objective meets the criteria to be a candidate for procedural analysis: it consists of a series of skills which must be performed in sequence although the learning of individual steps are not dependent on each other.

2. The instructor was then asked to visualize the performance and report each step. During this process, she found that it was useful to actually manipulate equipment. The initial set of steps were:

The student will

2(a) find a quiet environment

(b) find a clean counter

(c) obtain the Gravol (with the doctor's order sheet)

(d) obtain the needle lead, syringe, and alcohol swab

(e) open the needle package

(f) open the syringe package

(g) take the cap from the tip of the syringe

(h) put the needle head and syringe together

(i) open alcohol pack

(j) wipe off Gravol container (ampule)

(k) take cap from needle head and put down

(l) to take 1 c.c. from the ampule, put 1 c.c. of air into the ampule

(m) lift ampule in hand (needle in) and withdraw 1.1 c.c. of Gravol (not touching inner barrel of needle)

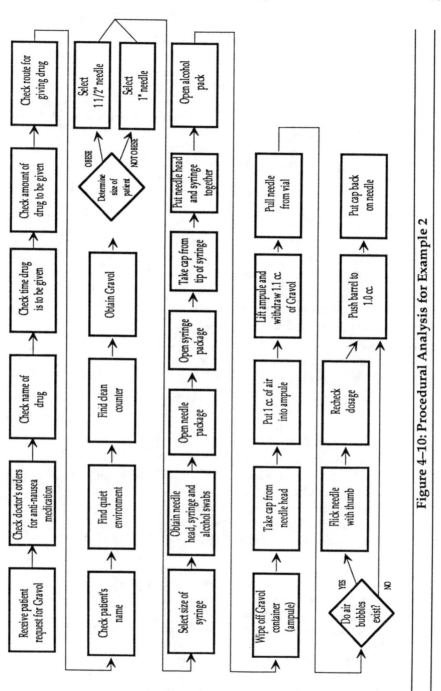

Figure 4–10: Procedural Analysis for Example 2

(n) pull needle from ampule, then check for air bubbles

(o) if air bubbles exist,

  (i) flick needle with thumb to remove them

  (ii) recheck dosage

  (iii) push barrel to 1.0 c.c. if no air bubbles exist

(p) put cap back on needle

3. When this list of behaviors was reviewed by the instructor, considering the input needed for each step and the output of the previous step, two gaps in the initial list were revealed. At the beginning of the task, it was decided that a series of safety checks had to be performed before the student started to prepare the equipment and medications. Second, before step 2(d) was performed, a judgement as to the size of the needle (based on physical characteristics of the patient) had to be made. The results of the review yielded:

The student will

2(a1) receive a patient request for Gravol

2(a2) check the doctor's orders for anti-nausea medication

2(a3) check the name of the drug

2(a4) check the time that the drug is to be given

2(a5) check the amount of the drug to be administered

2(a6) check the route (method) of giving the drug

2(a7) check the patient's name

2(a8) find a quiet environment (formerly 2d)

The procedure remains the same as the initial list until step 2(d), at which point the revision includes:

2(d1) determine the physical size of the patient

2(d2) if the patient is obese, select a 1 1/2" needle if the patient is not obese select a 1" needle

2(d3) based on the size of the needle and the amount of medication select the size of the syringe

2(d4) obtain needle lead, syringe, and alcohol swab (formerly 2d)

The procedure remains the same through step 2(p).

4. The observation of another individual performing the task did not yield further revisions.

5. The diagrammed procedural analysis appears in Figure 4-10.

6. The final step is to test the analysis in instruction and to determine whether or not further revision should be done, based on students' difficulties in mastering the objective.

Alternative Sequencing Principles

As was discussed in the previous sections, task analysis is an appropriate sequencing technique for high-level or complex learning, usually in the cognitive or the affective domain, and procedural analysis is useful for psychomotor tasks in which a number of behaviors must be performed in sequence. It is also possible of course to combine these two types of analysis, yielding a sequence of behaviors some of which are further analyzed hierarchically. There are, however, instructional situations in which neither of these approaches is useful. For example, one may be teaching several lower-level cognitive objectives (perhaps at the comprehension level), none of which are dependent on previous learning. Or a course may contain a series of application or analysis-level objectives, each analyzed separately, but with no inter-dependencies among them. In such cases it is still useful for both the instructor and the learners to have a clear sequencing plan; for the instructor this may simply be a management technique, and for the learner it will be an aid to the organization of materials, reading, and other activities. Dependent on the subject area and the level of the instruction, one or more of the following approaches may be appropriate.

Historical Sequence

In a course where the topics cover some time span and objectives tend to be at the same level of learning, it is common to organize the course in terms of the historical sequence of the events. For example, a session on the history of women might begin with the study of Hatsheput (1503-1482 B.C.), followed by the Byzantine empress, Theodora (A.D. 508-548), Isabella d'Este from Renaissance Italy (1474 to 1539), and so on. The use of historical sequence is a convenient way to organize the course, and it also adds to audience perception of the development of change in women's roles, which could be an overall instructional goal.

The subject area need not be historical to utilize this approach; an English literature course, a moral philosophy lecture, or an introductory workshop in psychology could as easily be organized in this fashion.

Content Relationships

Task analysis and procedural analysis are both concerned with the order in which activities or topics should be dealt with to facilitate learning. It is sometimes the case that even though this type of structure is not relevant, there are relationships among the concepts or topics in the course. An analysis of this type is called content analysis (cf. Sax, 1968, pp. 273-279). Briefly, the relationships among concepts are analyzed in terms of the associations among them; either degree of similarity or logi-

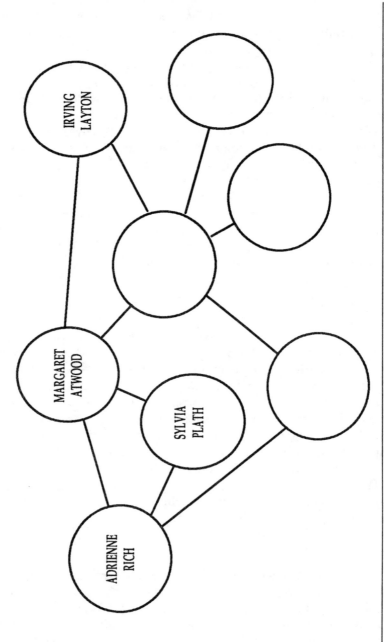

Figure 4–11: Content Analysis

cal relationship. For example, in the organization of a series on contemporary poetry, where there was no hierarchical structure among the objectives, the instructor could decide that the poetry of Adrienne Rich was more similar to that of Sylvia Plath than to Margaret Atwood, but all three were more similar to each other than to the poetry of Irving Layton. The topics could then be arranged so that the more similar poets' works were discussed in sequence. If desired, this type of analysis can also be diagrammed, with the distance between concepts in the diagram representing the degree of similarity (Figure 4-11).

The clusters of concepts or topics are then taught together. As with other kinds of sequencing principles, it is valuable to make this structure explicit, perhaps providing a copy of the diagram along with the objectives.

Classic or Traditional Groupings

In introductory or survey courses most objectives may often be at one level, for example, the comprehension level, with a few comparative or analysis-level objectives. There may, for example, be a series of objectives of the form, "The student will be able to describe the process of learning using behaviorist theory...using cognitive theory, etc." In survey courses in areas such as psychology, sociology, or English literature, there are often classic or traditional ways in which the field is divided. To illustrate, educational psychology has been grouped into the areas of developmental (child and adolescent) psychology, cognitive psychology, classroom processes, and measurement and evaluation. It then may be logical, if other approaches to instructional analysis are not appropriate, to organize a course entitled "Introduction to Educational Psychology" according to accepted subdivisions in the area. Again, learners should be aware of what this organization is, and why it was chosen.

Practical Sequencing

In professional training (nursing, social work, dentistry, etc.) or in laboratory situations, it may be the case that external variables influence or determine the sequence of instruction. Although a procedural or hierarchical analysis may be ideal in clinical teaching in a nursing course, the practical situation (what patients are on the floor, needs of the hospital staff) may, at least in part, determine the actual sequence of instruction. It was found, for example, in a recent survey (Kiely, 1981) that a nursing faculty used "specific needs of the patient" to sequence instruction 55.3% of the time. Similarly, an introductory course in social work theory may need to be organized so as to coincide with learners' field experiences as volunteer workers.

When a practical situation determines the sequence of instruction, particular care must be taken to ensure that the audience has the prerequisite skills for a particular situation. Although instruction may be, out of necessity, organized according to external variables, the learning to take place within situations may well be hierarchical or procedural.

CHAPTER FIVE

DEVELOPING THE INSTRUCTIONAL STRATEGY

by Patricia Cranton and Cynthia B. Weston

Once the content of a course or other segment of instruction has been described in terms of the expected learning and once that learning has been sequenced, the next step in planning instruction is the selection of the methods and materials of instruction. Although it may seem that this is an easy task primarily dictated by the subject area and the size of the class, there are several variables that should be considered in the selection of both methods (lectures, discussion groups, modularized instruction, simulations, etc.) and teaching materials (readings, films, videotapes, etc.). For over twenty years educational researchers have been investigating the degree to which different instructional techniques facilitate learning for individuals with different characteristics. Although this research is complex and has not met with complete success (cf. Cronbach, 1977), some general principles can be derived from the results obtained to date. As instructors we are all aware that we prefer to learn in certain ways (by discussing, at home with music in the background, by attending public lectures, etc.); it is logical that this is also the case for our audience. Some individuals learn most efficiently when they are given detailed guidelines or a structure for the learning process; others will achieve far more by working independently, with a given set of objectives, often devised by themselves. This is but one example of the way in which individuals' learning processes vary. The instructor who wishes to promote maximum learning must consider both the characteristics of the audience and the "external" variables of the instructional situation (group size, physical facilities, etc.).

One of the most common objections to the concept of matching instructional methods and materials to audience and situational characteristics is that since a typical group will be heterogeneous, it is not practical to design the instruction to meet the needs of all individuals. Of course, the ideal situation of one instructor working with one learner or a small homogeneous group of individuals is not often feasible, and as a result, compromises must be made. It is reasonable, however, to consider the abilities and preferences of learners in any group and, as much as possible, to incorporate appropriate techniques into the instruction. In general, this may be done in several ways: utilizing a variety of techniques so that at different times individuals are working in their preferred mode; tailoring instruction to the majority of the group (when there is a clear majority) and designing optional activities for other learners; and dividing the group into two or three sub-groups where, for example, one group does independent research, one works with programmed or computerized instruction, and one interacts directly with the instructor.

The second argument raised by most instructors is that the assessment of audience characteristics at the beginning of the session is not only time-consuming and difficult, but also results in near-impossible last-minute changes to the instructional plan. Indeed, it is generally not possible to administer a battery of personality and ability tests on the first day of class, to analyze and interpret these results, and to develop matching instructional techniques for the next class. On the other hand, some information (particularly past achievement or ability) is often available to the instructor in advance. Also, some of the most relevant characteristics can be measured quickly, and if optional instructional techniques have been prepared in advance, the adaptation to these characteristics can be relatively painless and quite rewarding. Many workshops, seminars, and professional development activities require advance registration. When this is the case, a short questionnaire can be included with the registration, asking for information about experience, other workshops or courses taken, preferred learning styles, and so on.

Instructors may be concerned that adaptation to individual differences will make it necessary to vary the evaluation techniques as well. How can a learner who completes an independent project be judged in the same way as someone who attends lectures and participates in discussion? It is true that if individuals are working toward different objectives, or towards objectives at different levels of learning, the format of the evaluation may vary, and this will lead the instructor to a criterion-referenced approach or contract grading (see Chapter Six). If institutional constraints do not allow for a criterion-referenced approach, and if all participants are required to learn the same set of objectives, they can be evaluated in the same way, regardless of the method by which they acquire the learning. For example, for the objective, "The student will be able to calculate three measures of central tendency for a given set of data," the individual who utilizes a computer assisted program and the person who attends a problem-solving seminar can both be evaluated using the same technique (probably a short-answer test).

In summary, it is usually possible to provide alternate forms of instruction for individuals with different characteristics when it is clear that this is required. This chapter will describe a variety of teaching methods, materials, or media for conveying information, considerations for the analysis of the audience, guidelines for selecting the appropriate methods and materials for specific instructional situations, and some general characteristics of effective instruction.

The distinction between instructional methods and materials is, at times, an arbitrary one. The use of programmed instruction, for example, could be described as a method, and obviously the programmed books or readings are materials. For the purpose of this chapter, instructional methods are defined as any means by which the instructor conveys the information required to master an objective. The method is the vehicle or technique for instructor-learner communication and not, it should be noted, the content of the communication. Materials, on the other hand, are the resources used to communicate information (for example, printed matter or audio-visual materials). We may, as instructors, tend to think of reading or the use of videotapes primarily as resources which can be used in such a variety of ways that they cannot be said to constitute a specific method.

Instructional Methods

Teaching methods can be described in at least four categories: (1) instructor-centered (that is, the majority of the information conveyed directly by the instructor); (2) interactive; (3) individualized techniques; and (4) experiential learning. Again, the categorization system may appear to be somewhat arbitrary; however each category reflects a primary characteristic of the methods which is relevant to situational and learner characteristics.

Instructor-Centered Methods

In the instructor-centered methods, the teacher is primarily responsible for conveying information to the audience; the direction of the communication tends to be one-way, from the instructor to the learner.

The most familiar of these methods is the *lecture*, in which one instructor speaks directly to an audience. The lecture is an efficient and effective method for instruction at the lower levels (knowledge and comprehension) of the cognitive domain, particularly for large groups. The major drawback of the lecture method is that learners are passive receivers of information; many types of learning require more extensive involvement on the part of the audience. It can also be appropriate for any of the higher levels of the cognitive domain and for some aspects of the affective domain, but in these cases should be accompanied by other methods which include audience participation in the learning process.

A second instructor-centered method is *questioning,* where the teacher directs a series of verbal questions to a series of individual learners or to the group as a whole, asking for volunteer responses. This technique is commonly combined with the lecture or other methods and is used either as a technique for monitoring learning, or as a form of "discovery learning" (where a well-planned sequence of questions leads individuals to the discovery of concepts, abstractions, or generalizations). Questioning is useful for instruction at most levels of the cognitive or affective domains but generally should be considered as a supplemental technique, unless the group is very small and the participation of all individuals is ensured. As a method for monitoring learning, questioning is almost always valuable, except when it is used with individuals who demonstrate anxiety or lack of self-confidence in speaking in a group. When used for discovery learning, questioning can be effective for most individuals but is also time-consuming and may be frustrating for those who prefer structure and organization.

Demonstration can be used in a variety of contexts. A concept, the application of a concept, or a psychomotor skill is illustrated by the instructor. This method is most appropriate at the higher levels of the cognitive domain, where the instructor may solve a mathematical problem on the chalkboard or write a computer program while the audience observes the process on a screen, and in the psychomotor domain, where the instructor may demonstrate a clinical skill or illustrate the correct racquet grip. Demonstration is, of course, almost always used in conjunction with other methods. It may be preceded by a short lecture and is often followed by an experiential method in which the learners practise the skill or procedure.

Interactive Methods

The interactive methods utilize communication among learners, as well as between instructor and learner. In general, learning is usually facilitated by active participation, and interaction or discussion can be an effective means of ensuring involvement in the learning process.

The most commonly used interactive method is *class discussion*. Given an issue, question, or topic of interest, learners discuss with each other their own points of view or relevant arguments. The instructor may participate in the discussion, usually in the role of a leader or manager (asking for clarification, summarizing major points, focussing on the issue, etc.). Class discussion is particularly effective for instruction in the upper levels of the cognitive domain (analysis, synthesis, and evaluation) and all levels of the affective domain. There are obvious practical limitations to the use of discussion. The group size must be small, at least less than 30, to ensure participation by all. If individuals have difficulty in expressing themselves or feel anxious about speaking in a group, they will not benefit from discussion. Also, when used extensively this technique can be time-consuming. However, in a summary of early research on class discussion versus the lecture method, McKeachie (1969) reports that in any comparative study which was concerned with higher-level cognitive learning or attitude and motivation, class discussion was found to be the superior method.

Discussion groups can be used in place of class discussions when the group is larger, when the learners' interests vary, or when members of the audience feel more comfortable interacting with a smaller number of individuals. Specific questions, issues, or topics of interest are chosen, and the group is divided into several smaller groups, usually with about three to seven people per group. Depending on the nature of the objective and the characteristics of the audience, the groups may be structured so that they are homogeneous in some way (for example, similarity of interest or background in a group), or they may be designed to be quite heterogeneous in order to promote exposure to different perspectives. Again, the group cannot be extremely large; even with fifty in the audience, the organization and management of ten groups can be awkward or confusing. Also, some individuals may be reluctant to participate due to anxiety, lack of self-confidence, etc., and the technique can be time-consuming. Discussion groups do facilitate learning in the upper levels of the cognitive domain and in all levels of the affective domain. They are particularly useful in the affective area where learners often have a variety of concerns, and individuals with common concerns can be grouped together.

Group projects are used when learners have similar or complementary interests, or when there is evidence that they will benefit from the interaction with their peers in the completion of a project. Individuals investigate a specific topic or issue, or they create a product either assigned by the instructor or selected according to their interests. The instructor acts as a consultant and manager of the learning process. This method is also most appropriate in the higher levels of each of the domains of learning and has the advantage of encouraging involvement in the learning process. The evaluation of learning can be more difficult, unless it is assumed that members of each group contribute and participate equally.

Peer teaching is a more structured interactive method and is particularly useful when extreme differences in ability level or past experience with the content exist within the group. In peer teaching (sometimes referred to as "learning cells"), individuals who have mastered the objective quickly or before entering the instruction, adopt the role of the instructor and teach the material to one, two, or three others who have not yet mastered it. The use of this method has several advantages. Individuals who would otherwise be bored while the instruction focussed on content with which they are familiar can be active and also reinforce their knowledge of the area. Also, it is often the case that a peer is more able to foresee the difficulties that an individual is having in the learning process than an instructor who is a subject area expert. Finally, instruction occurs in small groups or even individually, which is more likely to ensure the involvement of all participants. Some problems can be encountered in the use of this method. If the peer teachers are not completely competent in their mastery of the objective, their misconceptions or errors may be relayed to the other learners. And, of course, as we all know, competence in the subject area does not necessarily produce competence in instruction. To be effective, the process of peer teaching must be carefully planned and monitored by the instructor.

Individualized Learning Methods

Individualized learning techniques are based on the assumptions that individuals learn at different speeds and that regular immediate feedback facilitates the learning process. To some extent, the basis of these techniques lies in behaviorism: the early individualization techniques (teaching machines, programmed instruction) exhibit the small-step, shaping characteristics that are fundamental to that approach. Recently, the emphasis being placed by educational researchers on the investigation of individual differences continues to support this thinking, although it is now generally agreed that the learning process is more complex than the behaviorists originally allowed.

The individualized learning methods are those in which learners work directly with prepared materials at their own pace, receiving information as to their progress at regular intervals. Generally, learners are provided with quite structured materials, although this is not necessarily the case. The media used can vary: programmed instruction is usually printed material; modularized instruction a combination of media; and computerized instruction printed material on a screen, sometimes with graphics or audio supplements.

In *programmed instruction*, the content of an objective or set of objectives is broken into small, sequential steps: the learner is presented with some information, then answers a question based on that information. Depending on the answer, the learner turns to a specific page (this is referred to as "branching") and is either informed that the response is correct, or is given further information. The instruction is usually presented in a book or booklet and covers several objectives. The format of this technique restricts its use to the lower levels (knowledge, comprehension, and application) of the cognitive domain. Also students may respond negatively to the amount of structure in programmed instruction. The advantages of programmed instruction are: the individual is provided with considerable structure and is therefore not likely to experience failure; feedback as to the correctness of the response is provided immediately; and the learner is able to work at his or her own pace.

Modularized instruction includes a wide variety of presentation formats. Most commonly, the instruction centers around a booklet which may contain readings (or which may refer the learner to outside readings) and provides activities or exercises related to the readings. A module may also refer learners to audio or visual materials. Feedback can be provided within the module (with model answers), or the instructor can act as a tutor or advisor, answering questions and responding to written work. Within a course, modules can be used to teach all objectives or can be used as remedial, enrichment, or optional learning activities. Modularized instruction is particularly useful in courses where individuals have wide varieties of previous exposure to the area or where ability levels vary greatly. It can be used for instruction at all levels of the cognitive and affective domains. The benefits of modularized instruction are that individuals can be involved in a variety of activities; they can pursue specific interests of their own; and they are able to work at their own pace in the learning process. However, unless appropriate modules can be purchased, the development of the materials is very time-consuming for the instructor. Although the time commitment decreases considerably once the module is produced, the instructor must still act as a tutor, manager, and often, evaluator. Learners should be highly motivated and able to work independently, otherwise modular instruction can be a frustrating experience.

Computerized instruction can also take a variety of forms. The early "computer assisted instruction" resembled programmed instruction, except that the branching procedures were done by machine. It proved to be motivating and efficient at the lower levels of learning, but was not seen to be particularly cost effective. Simulations, games, and more interactive instruction (where learners were able to submit words, phrases, or, at times, sentences) allowed the educator to work with higher levels of learning, but the programming required is more complex and time-consuming for an instructor to undertake. Commercial programs, when they are appropriate to the objectives of the instruction, can be very effective. However, with the advent of microcomputers and their steadily decreasing cost and increasing capabilities, computerized instruction, in a variety of formats, is available to many instructors.

There are two general ways in which the computer is used in the learning process. In the first, which more closely resembles the original uses of the computer, the individual interacts with a program that has been written or purchased by the instructor. Usually, information is displayed in some way, either printed material on a screen or through graphic or audio media. The learner then answers questions or solves problems and submits the responses, most often by means of a normal keyboard, to the machine. Immediate feedback is provided on the response. The branching techniques used in programmed instruction can be much more sophisticated with the use of a computer; also different versions of an instructional program can be easily designed for individuals with different learning styles or abilities. The second increasingly common use of the computer in instruction is that of learning by programming. For example, it has been shown that young children quickly learn geometric principles, using a simple language called LOGO, where they instruct a "turtle" (either a mechanical turtle or a marker on a screen) to move according to various rules in order to draw shapes. At higher levels of instruction, individuals learn mathematical or statistical principles by writing their own programs to solve problems, and in other subject areas (e.g. economics, physics, environmental sciences, etc.), participants learn by developing their own simulations in which various principles are applied to case studies or practical situations.

For some individuals using the computer produces a high anxiety level which detracts from their learning. In general, the major disadvantage, however, of computerized instruction is the amount of instructor time and effort which must go into the development and management of either the programs or the "projects."

However, computerized instruction has several advantages: learners are able to interact individually with the instructional material while working at their own pace; immediate feedback is provided; working with the computer is motivating for many individuals; and learners who have difficulty interacting with their peers or feel anxious about performing in front of others are able to work independently while receiving the benefits of the interaction with the machine.

Experiential Learning Methods

A great deal of learning, particularly in the affective and psychomotor domains, takes place in situations where the participant is actually involved in performing tasks. In physical education, individuals learn tennis, physical fitness, basketball, etc., by actually participating in activities and games. In professional training, student nurses learn to administer IVs, make beds, and interact with patients while they are working in the clinical area. In education, one component of teacher training is always student teaching, or actually performing in front of a class, with the assistance of a master or supervising teacher. This category of instructional methods can be labelled as experiential, since learning is facilitated by experiencing or doing. Although they usually take place outside of the traditional classroom, methods such as role-playing and simulations may also be viewed as experiential, since the learner is directly participating in a realistic and practical situation.

Experiential methods can also be described in terms of each of the categories discussed so far; that is, they may be instructor-centered (as in a physical education drill where participants perform exercises in unison with the instructor), interactive (as in team sports or games), or individualized (as in laboratory projects). It is the unique characteristic of the individual performing in a real or simulated setting which distinguishes the experiential methods from the previous categories.

Field or clinical methods take place in natural settings such as hospitals, schools, social service agencies, or during sport competitions. The nature of the instruction is, of course, affected by the other participants in the setting (patients, staff, clients, competitors), and some of the principles of instructional design discussed so far (e.g. sequencing) have to be modified according to the requirements of the setting. Clinical or field teaching usually takes place while the learner is actually performing in the natural setting, or depending on the situation, after the performance has taken place. The learner is given a specific task or series of tasks to perform and, under the observation of the instructor, carries out these tasks. In situations where instructor observation is not practical, the learner is most commonly asked to report, after the performance, what has been done. Learning, then, is taking place by doing the task and receiving feedback on the performance from the instructor.

The major disadvantage of clinical or field teaching, from the instructor's point of view, is the evaluation of performance. The evaluation techniques are difficult to construct and are often subjective. In addition, the instruction itself requires a great deal of flexibility on the part of the instructor as the content of the session must be based on the needs of the situation. Advance planning and detailed management techniques are required. On the other hand, this technique has obvious advantages: the participant is actively involved in the learning process; feedback on the learner's performance is regularly and often immediately provided; and, the learning experience accurately represents the situations in which the individual will be performing after completion of the course.

In the psychomotor and affective domains, clinical or field teaching is often the ideal method for facilitating learning.

In *laboratory methods*, learners are still able to perform in situations which are realistic, but also where the consequences of their performance are carefully controlled by the instructor. Although we tend to associate the laboratory method with chemistry or physics, this technique is used in a variety of subject areas. In statistics, the learner can work with the computer to solve problems; in social work, participants can act out and videotape their interactions with pseudo-clients, and this can be viewed as the laboratory method.

The laboratory method can be used for the upper levels of the cognitive domain (application and above) and for all levels of the affective and psychomotor domains. It is particularly appropriate when the skills being taught cannot be applied in real situations, either for practical or safety reasons.

The disadvantages of this technique are similar to those listed for field or clinical teaching: evaluation of performance is difficult; and the advance planning for the instructional situation must be detailed.

The advantages of the laboratory method are: the learner is actively involved in the task which is being learned; the situation usually closely resembles the situation in which the skill will be used; and, feedback from the situation is often immediate.

Role-playing is commonly used in situations where participants are learning interpersonal skills, although it can be effectively used in other areas, such as in the upper levels of the cognitive domain. In role playing, participants act out a particular situation, practising the skills being mastered. For example, individuals studying social work may use role-playing to review interactions that they have had with clients during their volunteer field work. Although this method overlaps the previously discussed laboratory method and the use of simulations, it can be seen as a more specific form of each and is commonly enough used to warrant particular mention.

Role-playing has the advantage of allowing the participant to experience a variety of situations while remaining in a safe environment; as such it is extremely useful for the higher levels of the affective domain and aspects of the psychomotor domain, such as non-verbal communication. As with the other experiential learning methods, a drawback of the technique can be the difficulties arising in evaluation of learning.

Simulations and games can be used in all three domains of learning, usually for the higher levels of learning. Simulations accurately represent real situations and are commonly used to facilitate practice of the application of rules or principles to the situations, while remaining in a safe or practical environment. In medical training, for example, learners might practice diagnosis skills or be evaluated on their diagnoses using simulated patients. In teacher training, students often practice specific skills (such as leading discussions) in a simulated situation called microteaching. In a short teaching demonstration (5 or 10 minutes), students use one or two skills, with a small number of their peers acting as a class.

Games are used in a similar way to simulations; however they provide a more abstract representation of a real situation, and games are usually defined as having winners and losers and have more structured, artificial rules. As a result, games can be used to teach a wider variety of types of learning.

For those individuals who lack self-confidence or possess a high level of anxiety, games or simulations can produce debilitating reactions. However, the major benefit of simulations and games is the stimulation of interest and motivation. Also, learners are actively participating in the instructional process and are able to see the direct consequences of their decisions or behavior.

Finally, some forms of *drill* can be categorized as experiential learning, particularly in the psychomotor domain. In tennis instruction, for example, the learner may be required to repeat a forehand swing many times, using either a mechanical device to send the balls or working independently against a practice wall. The drills used in psychomotor learning are often more complex than this example, providing practice in a series of skills or a combination of skills. Drill is often the only method for teaching basic psychomotor skills which will be repeated many times as a part of more complex performances.

Drills are used similarly, although less frequently, in the other domains of learning. We probably all remember the basic arithmetic or spelling drills where the repetition of the response was designed to produce an automatic student response. And this method continues to be effective for the lower levels of the cognitive domain. Although it may not be a common or even acceptable instructional method, changes in attitude or affective learning will take place as a result of repetition of stimulus and response; positive examples can be found in behavior therapy where individuals are repeatedly exposed to anxiety-provoking situations and practise relaxed responses.

Summary

A variety of the more commonly used instructional methods have been briefly described. Table 5-1 provides a summary of those methods discussed along with some distinguishing features of each. As has been discussed, the selection of teaching methods is extremely complex and will be elaborated on later in the chapter (pp. 113 to 130).

Materials

Implicit in the discussion of teaching methods are teaching materials. The materials used when lecturing are often handouts, overhead transparencies, and certainly, oral presentation. The materials used in demon-

TABLE 5–1: Summary of Instructional Methods

INSTRUCTOR CENTERED	INTERACTIVE	INDIVIDUALIZED
Lecture - students are passive - efficient for lower levels of learning and large classes	**Class Discussion** - class size must be small - may be time-consuming - encourages student involvement	**Programmed Instruction** - most effective at lower learning levels - very structured - students work at own pace - students receive extensive feedback
	Discussion Groups - class size should be small - students participate - effective for high levels of cognitive learning and affective learning	**Modularized Instruction** - can be time-consuming - very flexible formats - students work at own pace
Questioning - monitors student learning - encourages student involvement - may cause anxiety for some		
Demonstration -illustrates an application of a skill or concept - students are passive	**Peer Teaching** - requires careful planning and monitoring - utilizes differences in student expertise - encourages student involvement	**Independent Projects** - most appropriate at higher levels of learning - can be time-consuming - students are actively involved in learning
	Group Projects - requires careful planning, including evaluation techniques - useful at higher levels of learning - encourages active student participation	**Computerized Instruction** - may involve considerable instructor-time or expense - can be very flexible - students work at own pace - students may be involved in varying activities

EXPERIENTIAL LEARNING METHODS			
Field or Clinical - occurs in natural setting during performance - students are actively involved - management and evaluation may be difficult	**Role Playing** - effective in affective and psychomotor domains - provides "safe" experiences - active student participation	**Simulations and Games** - provide practice of specific skills - produce anxiety for some students - active student participation	**Drill** - most appropriate at lower learning levels - provides active practice - may not be motivating for some students
Laboratory - requires careful planning and evaluation - students actively involved in a realistic setting			

strations are often real things or models of real objects. When it is determined that some individual study in the form of reading assignments is essential to instruction, then text materials become part of the method. Art history teachers often assign individual study of art prints and also often use slides during lectures. In this case, still pictures, in the form of prints and projected slides, are the materials included as part of the teaching method. In the following section, the characteristics of teaching materials will be discussed, as well as advantages and disadvantages of each. Additionally, criteria for selecting materials will be described.

Materials or Media

It may seem that the materials listed above fall into two categories— teaching materials and media. Handouts, text readings, and art prints might commonly be termed teaching materials, while overhead transparencies or slides might commonly be called media. This is an artificial distinction. Teaching materials include any resources that you use to present stimuli to the learner. Media can be defined in the same way. The individual delivering a lecture, the textbook, the art print, and the video-tape are all media of communication or ways of presenting stimuli to the learner. Materials or media? The answer must be that they are one and the same. The terms will be used interchangeably here, though there is some preference for the term "material" because it does not carry the multitude of often conflicting connotations associated with the word "media."

Three Components of Materials

The materials used to communicate an instructional message have three components in common: 1) a delivery system, 2) a message, and 3) a condition of abstraction. Each of these components will be discussed.

Delivery system. When you say that you will use handouts, overhead transparencies, readings, slides, computer assisted instruction (CAI), or audio tape, you are specifying only the delivery system of the teaching materials. A delivery system can be thought of as the physical form of the materials and the hardware which are used to present stimuli to the learner. The delivery system of a lecture is a person. Overhead transparencies (physical form of the material) and the overhead projector (hardware) are a delivery system, as are slides and a slide projector, audiotape and an audio tape player, or the paper and ink of a textbook. What is the handout, overhead transparency, textbook, or audiotape about? It could be anything from an interview with Castro to an identification of the four food groups. Saying that a textbook or film will be used as teaching materials tells us something about the delivery system—the shape, size, and equipment necessary—but really tells us nothing about the content.

Content or message. The information that is communicated with teaching materials is the content or the message. It seems pretty obvious that just specifying "textbook" doesn't indicate the content of the text. One must say that the textbook is about educational psychology, the videotape is about effectiveness of instructional television, or the slides are about impressionism. Teaching materials are used because they support, expand, or are in some way related to overall instruction. They present information that is relevant to the achievement of objectives.

Form or Condition of Abstraction. The form of the message is often the most important consideration when selecting or developing instructional materials, and yet it is the aspect of materials that is most often ignored. The form of the message contained in the textbook, slides, etc., can be thought of as occurring along a continuum from concrete (real things) to abstract (symbols). Let's take the topic of the bones of the human skeleton. The most concrete form of stimuli that can be used to deliver information about bones of the skeleton is an actual skeleton. This *real thing* is three-dimensional and naturally has all the characteristics of size, color, texture, weight, structure, flexibility, etc. The instructor might also use a *model* of the skeleton. The model is still three-dimensional and of actual size, but it is a plastic replica or an imitation and therefore has lost some of the actual characteristics of real bones. The weight, texture, or structure may differ. The color may be off, and the plastic bones may be less brittle than real bones. The learners will not find all of the characteristics of real bones in these imitations. The instructor might say, "A real bone, when cut in half would reveal an ossified structure, whereas you will notice that this plastic bone is solid when cut in half." The learners cannot see the ossified structure and are therefore being forced to imagine this or to deal with ossification on an abstract level. Because of this loss of realism, models are less concrete on the continuum. The instructor could also present the study of bones of the human skeleton by using pictures of a real skeleton. Many characteristics of the real thing are now absent. The learners cannot touch the bones to feel the weight or texture. The pictures are not actual size, nor is the color realistic. There are only two rather than three dimensions. Pictures are *illusions* of the real thing. The form of the message has become less realistic and more abstract. More abstract still are drawings of the skeleton. Certain details are left out and some details highlighted. A full color drawing, with natural shading, perspective, etc., is more concrete than a black and white line drawing of the bones of the skeleton. But these drawings are still *illusions* in that they only resemble the real thing.

FORMS	CONCRETE			ABSTRACT
	Real Things	Imitations	Illusions	Symbols
EXAMPLES	actual skeleton	plastic model of skeleton	photograph / drawing	words describing skeleton

Figure 5–1: Forms of Instructional Materials: The Concrete—Abstract Continuum

Finally, the learners can read about the bones of the skeleton. Words are merely *symbols* that have been designated as representations of objects or ideas. Symbols bear no resemblance to the real thing. They are the most abstract form in which a message can be presented to learners.

Components: Summary. To summarize, all instructional materials have three components:

1. Delivery system—the physical format and hardware necessary to use the materials (e.g. a person, a book, slides and projectors, film and projector, chalkboard).

2. Message—the content or information being conveyed.

3. Form or condition of abstraction—materials can be placed along a continuum from concrete to abstract, according to the form of the message. At least four overlapping categories can be identified along this continuum (see Figure 5-1):

a) Real things—fully dimensional, actual objects

b) Imitations—three-dimensional imitations (e.g. models)

c) Illusions—two-dimensional representations of real things (e.g. pictures, moving or still, audiotape or real sounds)

d) Symbols—abstract referents (e.g. written or spoken words, numbers, written musical notes)

It may appear that concrete forms of the message are being advocated. This is not the case. In the section on materials selection these forms will be discussed in terms of their specific application to the objectives. The forms are presented as alternatives; there are no preferences. The deci-

Table 5–2: Delivery System and Form of Twelve Common Instructional Materials

FORM		CHALK-BOARD	TEXT	SPECIMEN	MODEL	ORAL PRESENTA-TION	OVERHEAD TRANS-PARENCY
	DELIVERY SYSTEM	- board - chalk	- paper - ink			- person	- 8 1/2 x 11 transparency - overhead projector
	Real Things	NO	NO	YES	NO	NO	NO
	Imitations	NO	NO	NO	YES	NO	NO
	Illusions	e.g. - drawings	- pictures - drawings	NO	NO	NO	- drawings
	Symbols	e.g. - words (v) - numbers (v)	- words (v) - numbers (v) - charts (v) - graphs (v)	NO	NO	- words (a)	- words (v) - numbers (v) - charts (v) - graphs (v)

FORM		FLAT PHOTO-GRAPHS	SLIDES	FILM	VIDEOTAPE	AUDIOTAPE	COMPUTER-IZED
	DELIVERY SYSTEM	- photographic paper - paper & ink	- 2 x 2 slide - slide projector	- 8 mm, 16 mm film - projector	- 1/2", 3/4" videotape - videotape player - tv, monitor	- 1/8", 1/4" audiotape - tape player	- computer - disk & drive - keyboard - monitor - video interface - slide interface
	Real Things	NO	NO	NO	NO	NO	NO
	Imitations	NO	NO	- 3-D graphics	- 3-D graphics	NO	- 3-D graphics
	Illusions	e.g. - pictures	- pictures - drawings	- pictures - drawings - sounds (a)	- pictures - drawings - sounds (a)	- live sounds (a) - sound effects (a)	- pictures - drawings - sounds (a)
	Symbols	e.g. - words (v) - numbers (v) (if labelled)	- words - numbers (v) - charts (v) - graphs (v)	- words (a & v) - numbers (v) - charts (v) - graphs (v)	- words (a & v) - numbers (v) - charts (v) - graphs (v)	- words (a)	- words (a + v) - numbers (v) - charts (v) - graphs (v)

Note: (v) denotes visual stimuli; (a) denotes auditory stimuli

sion to use symbols, illusions, imitations, or the real things must be based on specific selection criteria: the nature of the learning, the composition of the audience, and the constraints of the instructional situation.

It should also be noted that the skeleton example allowed discussion of a variety of messages, ranging from presentation techniques to the real thing to verbal description. This would not be possible with many topics, such as the writing style of Charles Dickens. Writing, by definition, deals in symbols. There is not a concrete or real thing, other than the words themselves.

Thinking of instructional materials in terms of their three components is useful for several reasons. It emphasizes that one must consider not only the content or message that will be presented, but also the form in which it will be presented. It also emphasizes the wide range of materials, in various forms, from which one can choose when designing instruction. Finally, selecting appropriate materials, in terms of their delivery system and form, can aid in the achievement of objectives. This final point will be discussed in greater detail in the section on matching materials to instruction.

Table 5-2 presents some common classroom materials and, for each, indicates the message form it can present to the learner and the delivery system involved. This table may clarify the distinction between form or condition of abstraction and delivery system. In addition, it may be helpful when selecting material for instruction. For example, if you determine that illusions are a desirable way of presenting stimuli to the learner, reference to this table will indicate those materials that can provide illusions (e.g. pictures of various kinds).

Sensory stimuli. You will probably notice that the instructional materials in Table 5-2 fall largely into the illusion and symbol categories. With the exception of real things and imitations, our primary communication media in instruction are illusions and symbols. This means that we primarily present auditory and visual stimuli to the learners. Illusions can be visual (e.g. drawings and pictures) and auditory (e.g. tape of live sounds and sound effects). Symbols can also be visual (e.g. printed words and numbers) and auditory (e.g. spoken words).

Real things allow stimulation of additional senses. They can provide olfactory (smell), gustatory (taste), and tactile (touch) stimuli, as well as visual and auditory stimuli. When presented with a real skeleton, for example, the students can see and feel the bones. They can also hear sounds made by the bone when tapped on any hard surface, and they can even smell and taste the bones, if they are so inclined. Present them with illusions (pictures, still or moving, or drawings) and the learners will only be able to see the bones of the skeleton. They may also be given a written description (visual symbols) or a spoken description (auditory symbols).

Imitations, such as models, can also provide olfactory, gustatory, tactile, auditory, and visual stimuli. Models, by definition, are not the real thing, so some of the stimuli may not be realistic (e.g. the smell, taste, or feel may be unnatural).

Real things and models also allow for appreciation of dimensionality. To perceive the dimensions of objects we can move our heads, physically move around, or manipulate the object in order to gain various angles of view. This cannot be done with still pictures; however, several forms of moving illusions (e.g. video and film images) can provide partial appreciation of dimensionality. While we cannot manipulate or move around flat, two-dimensional visual images, the camera can act as our head and body by showing an object from several angles and distances. Within this two-dimensional frame we are given an illusion of three-dimensions. Computer graphics can produce two-dimensional images which rotate in such a way as to create an overwhelming 3-D effect. Once again, the dimension cannot be physically appreciated, but the viewers are often offered angles and views impossible in the real world. The structure of a molecule, for example, can be shown in various scales and perspectives that could not be seen with the human eye. Even a plastic model of a molecule has limitations that are overcome with computer graphics. It is because of this unique ability to construct a three-dimensional space that computer generated graphics are indicated as imitations as well as illusions on Table 5-2 (see CAI, film, videotape). These graphics are not imitations according to earlier criteria, as they are not actually three-dimensional; however, they do present a unique appreciation of dimensionality.

Description of Materials

Instructional materials have been discussed in terms of three components with emphasis on the degree of abstraction each stimulus presents to the learner. Materials will now be considered in terms of four instructional factors: associated method, pacing, group size, and interaction.

1. Associated Method refers to the instructional technique which most often incorporates the material. Materials are used within the context of one of the instructional methods discussed in an earlier section: instructor-centered, interactive, individualized, and experiential.

2. Pacing, or the rate at which information is presented to the learner, can be controlled by:

    a) presenter, (e.g. a lecture is paced by the speaker)

    b) learner, (e.g. reading of a textbook is done at the reader's pace)

    c) producer, here used as a general term to refer to those who were responsible for placing images and/or sound onto film or tape. The pace of information in these formats is determined by the designer, director, or producer.

3. Group size refers to the optimal size of the group with whom the material should be used. Many materials are quite flexible, such as slide-tape units, in that they can be used by individuals in a library carrel or shown to a large group.

4. Interaction refers to the potential of the material to respond or react variably to learners and to require a response from the learner. An easy way to conceive of interaction is to consider that the material in question and the learner are closed in a room together with no instructor available to respond to questions. With this in mind it becomes clear that a chalkboard on which an outline has been written cannot interact with the learner. An oral presentation, on the other hand, is delivered by a person and therefore has unlimited potential for responding and reacting to the learner in verbal and non-verbal ways. Practise questions and feedback which are commonly included in text and audio-visual materials are not included in this definition of interaction, as the response does not have the potential to be variable from learner to learner. Also, it is entirely possible for an individual to avoid responding to these questions; for example, the learner can continue reading or continue to listen to a language tape without responding in the expected manner. Materials are presented separately in the following discussion in order to isolate characteristics but are often used in combination during instruction. Table 5-3 summarizes the characteristics of common materials.

Oral presentation. The oral presentation of information is probably the most commonly used instructional material. The inclusion of oral presentation will overlap with what you have read in the section on the description of methods, but it is included here to emphasize that the use of spoken verbal symbols is as much an instructional material as an overhead transparency and should be regarded as a material option, not a given.

TABLE 5–3: Comparison of Common Instructional Materials

MATERIAL	ASSOCIATED METHODS	GROUP SIZE					PACING
		1	2-14	15-30	31-50	50 +	
LIVE: ORAL PRESENTATION	Instructor Centered						
	a) lecture		*	**	**	***	Presentor
	b) questioning		**	***			
	c) demonstration accompanied by oral presentation	**	***	*			
	Interactive						Presentor &/or Learner
	a) class discussion		***	**	*		
	b) group discussion		*	***	**		Learner
CHALKBOARD	Instructor Centered						Presentor (when writing) & learner (visual review)
	a) lecture		**	***	*		
	Interactive						
	a) class discussion		***	**	*		
TEXT	Individualized						Learner
	a) programmed	***	*				
	b) modularized	***	*				
SPECIMEN	Instructor Centered						Presentor
	a) lecture		**	*			
	b) demonstration	**	***				
	Experiential						Learner
	a) field or clinical	***	*				
	b) laboratory	***	*				

INTERACTION	ADVANTAGES	DISADVANTAGES
VARIABLE: minimum to maximum verbal and non-verbal response	1. High potential for interaction 2. Easy to create; can use notes or be extemporaneous 3. Inexpensive 4. Good for large groups 5. No equipment necessary	1. Primarily verbal abstractions 2. Spoken words are transient. Learner must exercise short-term memory to keep words and ideas in mind until sentence is finished & ideas can be comprehended. 3. Difficult to repeat ideal presentations
NONE	1. Easy to use 2. No technical expertise necessary (although legible handwriting is important) 3. Inexpensive 4. Color can be used when necessary	1. Presentor's back is turned toward audience 2. Board space can be poorly used and random notes can be confusing to learners 3. Irrelevant information which remains in view can be distracting 4. Information must be rewrittten or redrawn for each use
NONE	1. Learners pace rate of information acquisition 2. Learners create own word emphasis, tone, etc. 3. Permanence allows for repeated review 4. Consistent. Students in various classes & years receive identical information 5. Reusable	1. Abstract symbols may be difficult for some learners 2. Poorly duplicated materials can be difficult to read; images difficult to see
VARIABLE: -inanimate tend not to be responsibe - animate can be fully responsive	1. Learners get direct, concrete experience 2. Can stimulate all the senses	1. Some real things are difficult to transport to classroom 2. Can be expensive to provide specimens for individual use

Legend for group size: * - ok; ** - good; *** - optimal

TABLE 5–3: Comparison of Common Instructional Materials (continued)

MATERIAL	ASSOCIATED METHODS	GROUP SIZE 1	2-14	15-30	31-50	50 +	PACING
MODEL	Instructor Centered a) lecture		**	*			Presentor
	b) demonstration	**	***	---	---	---	
	Experiential a) laboratory	***	**				Learner (when mastery is critical)
	b) simulation	***	**	---	---	---	Presentor (when time is critical)
OVERHEAD TRANS-PARENCIES	Instructor Centered a) lecture		*	**	**	***	Presentor
	Interactive a) class discussion		**	***	*		Learner (visual review)
AUDIOTAPE RECORDINGS	Instructor Centered a) lecture		*	**	**	***	Producer
	Individualized a) programmed	***	*				
	b) modularized	***	*	---	---	---	

INTERACTION	ADVANTAGES	DISADVANTAGES
VARIABLE: from non-responsive to very responsive	1. Learners receive direct concrete experience 2. Can stimlate all relevant senses 3. Can be designed to present a controlled experience (e.g., simulators)	1. Can be expensive to create 2. Can be expensive to operate
NONE	1. Presentor faces audience while writing or displaying information 2. Can be used with large groups (because projection enlarges the image) 3. Can be used with lights on for notetaking 4. Can be prepared in advance 5. Are reusable 6. Can direct learner's attention by turning light on and off 7. Can be prepared using simple techniques (e.g., handlettering, typewriter)	1. Should not be used to display pages of text. Present only *one* idea per transparency. 2. Image is visible only while light is on. Information is not as transient as spoken words, but is more transient than text or chalkboard. 3. Requires special equipment 4. Some skill required for preparation
NONE	1. Can bring otherwise inaccesible auditory experiences into classroom (e.g., the London Symphony) 2. Consistent information presented the same way every time 3. Reusable 4. Can be replayed for review 5. Equipment is easy to operate	1. Primarily verbal abstraction 2. Spoken words are transient 3. Producers predetermine pace 4. Producers predetermine tone (emphasis and interpretation) 5. Requires special equipment

Legend for group size: * - ok; ** - good; *** - optimal

TABLE 5–3: Comparison of Common Instructional Materials (continued)

MATERIAL	ASSOCIATED METHODS	GROUP SIZE 1	2-14	15-30	31-50	50 +	PACING
PHOTOGRAPHS	Instructor Centered						
	a) lecture		**	*			
	------------------	---	---	---	---	---	Presentor
	b) questioning		**	*			
	Interactive						
	a) class discussion		**	*			Presentor
	------------------	---	---	---	---	---	-------------
	b) group discussion		**	*			Learner
	Individualized						
	a) programmed	***	*				
	------------------	---	---	---	---	---	Learner
	b) modularized	***	*				
SLIDES	Instructor Centered						
	a) lecture		*	**	***	***	
	------------------	---	---	---	---	---	Presentor
	b) questioning		**	***	*		
	Individualized						
	a) modularized	***	**				Learner
FILMSTRIPS	Instructor Centered						
	a) lecture		*	**	***	**	Presentor
	------------------	---	---	---	---	---	
	b) questioning		**	***	*		
	Individualized						
	a) modularized	***	**				Learner

INTERACTION	ADVANTAGES	DISADVANTAGES
NONE	1. Can bring otherwise inaccessible visual experiences into classroom (e.g., underwater world) 2. Individual use permits learner pacing & review 3. Are reusable 4. No equipment necessary	1. Cannot be used with large groups 2. Cannot be used to show motion 3. Photos large enough for use with more than 15 students are very expensive 4. Special skills required to produce photographs
NONE	1. Can bring otherwise inaccessible visual experiences into classroom 2. Can be used with very large groups 3. Individual use permits learner pacing & review 4. Used in dark room which focuses attention on the screen 5. Are reusable 6. Can be easily rearranged 7. Motion can be simulated by showing a series of slides in rapid succession	1. Poorly suited to display of more than 15-20 words or simple graphs/charts 2. Shown in darkened room which interferes with note-taking & discussion 3. Requires special equipment 4. Special skills required to produce
NONE	1. Can bring otherwise inaccessible visual experiences into classroom 2. Can be used with very large groups 3. Individual use permits learner pacing & review 4. Used in dark room which focuses attention on the screen 5. Are reusable	1. Images are in a fixed sequence which limits flexibility 2. Format makes film vulnerable to scratches 3. Poorly suited to display of more than 15-20 words or simple graphs/charts 4. Shown in darkened room which interferes with note-taking & discussion 5. Requires special equipment 6. Special skills required to produce

Legend for group size: * - ok; ** - good; *** - optimal

TABLE 5-3: Comparison of Common Instructional Materials (continued)

MATERIAL	ASSOCIATED METHODS	GROUP SIZE 1	2-14	15-30	31-50	50 +	PACING
SLIDE/ FILMSTRIP & AUDIO COMBINATIONS	Instructor Centered a) lecture		*	* *	* * *	* * *	Producer
	Individualized a) modularized	* * *	* *				
FILM	Instructor Centered a) lecture ------------------ b) demonstration	 - - - 	 * * - - - * *	 * * - - - * *	 * * * - - - * * *	 * * * - - - * * *	Producer
	Individualized a) modularized	* * *	* *				

INTERACTION	ADVANTAGES	DISADVANTAGES
NONE	1. Information is presented visually & aurally 2. Includes all advantages of slides/filmstrips & audiotape 3. Well-suited to bilingual situations since different audio tracks can be prepared 4. Consistent presentation of information 5. Reusable	1. Pace is predetermined 2. Tone is predetermined 3. Shown in darkened room which interferes with note-taking & discussion 4. Review of sections of program is difficult. If tape is rewound or visuals advanced, synchronization is easily lost 5. Special equiment required 6. Special skills required to produce

NONE	1. Can show motion
	  - realistic
	  - slow motion
	  - time lapse (speeded up)
	
	2. Can bring unusal experiences into classroom including events that are imperceptible to human eye (e.g. a plant growing)
	
	3. Audio & visual information
	
	4. Can be used with large groups
	
	5. Use in darkened room focuses attention on screen
	
	6. Consistent
	
	7. Reusable
		1. Pace is predetermined
		
		2. Tone is predetermined
		
		3. Difficult to rewind to show a segment out of sequence
		
		4. Special equipment required
		
		5. Considerable expertise necessary to produce
		
		6. Can be expensive to purchase
		
		7. Shown in darkened room which interferes with note-taking & discussion

Legend for group size: * - ok; ** - good; *** - optimal

TABLE 5-3: Comparison of Common Instructional Materials (continued)

MATERIAL	ASSOCIATED METHODS	GROUP SIZE					PACING
		1	2-14	15-30	31-50	50+	
VIDEOTAPE RECORDINGS	Instructor Centered						
	a) lecture		***	**	*		Producer
	- - - - - - - - - - - -	---	---	---	---	---	
	b) demonstration		***	**	*		
	Individualized						
	a) modularized	***	**				
COMPUTERIZED MATERIALS	Individualized						
	a) computerized	***	*				Producer (when speed is crucial)
	Experiential						
	a) simulation games	***	*				Learner (when mastery is primary concern)
	b) drills	***	*				

INTERACTION	ADVANTAGES	DISADVANTAGES
NONE	1. Can show motion 2. Can bring unusual experiences into classroom 3. Audio & visual information 4. Ease of use facilitates individual use 5. Easy to rewind & access discrete segments 6. Consistent 7. Reusable recordings 8. Can be used in normally lit room 9. Moderately easy to produce 10. Can be played back immediately 11. Tapes can be re-recorded	1. Small size of tv screen limits use with groups of more than 30 2. Pace & tone are predetermined 3. Image quality not as good as film for fine detail
VARIABLE: From limited to very responsive	1. CAI is individualized 2. Can be highly interactive 3. Can provide visual & auditory stimuli 4. Can present stills & moving pictures 5. Can provide color 6. Can provide dimensionality in graphic displays 7. Reusable	1. One keyboard and/or computer is necessary for each student 2. Expertise required to create programs

Legend for group size: * - ok; ** - good; *** - optimal

Chalkboard. The chalkboard is also a very commonly used instructional material. In conjunction with a lecture or discussion, it is often used in two ways. One use is to place on the board, in advance, words and/or drawings which will remain visible throughout the session. Words and images which remain visible can act as organizers, for example, an outline of topics or activities, or a drawing which acts as an organizer for a discussion of its parts. While the accompanying oral presentation may be presenter-paced, the learners can use the board as a reference. Chalkboards can also be used progressively during a presentation, as when something is drawn to illustrate an immediate point or when verbal cues are placed on the board as points are covered. Once again, this is presenter-paced, as the information is written on the board, with some learner pacing possible in the visual review of information.

Text. Texts and other printed materials have been relied upon as instructional materials for years. The primary advantage of printed materials is that they allow the learner to determine the pace of information presentation. Individuals with different reading speeds and abilities can proceed at their own pace, can reread and review text and pictures, and can access whatever portion of text they desire (e.g. they can read the conclusions before the introduction). Text materials are usually used individually, though occasionally pages are projected to a group for joint reading. Individual pacing will be modified with group reading.

Specimens and models. Specimens and models serve a similar instructional function and therefore will be treated jointly. Specimens include such real things as microscopic creatures used in zoology, a camera used in a photography workshop, an actual patient on which a nurse practices or applies skills, or an actual plane flown by the pilot in training. Models might include a plastic representation of a DNA structure used in biology, a cut-away replica of a carburetor for auto mechanics, or the life-like mannequins used in many cardio-pulmonary resuscitation (CPR) sessions. Both specimens and models offer direct experience to the learner. Real things have certain advantages, because they retain all of the realistic cues. However, in some cases, imitations are more appropriate instructional materials, because they can offer a unique view (e.g. cross-section of the earth's crust), or only a controlled experience (CPR practice on a simulated victim, pilot training in flight simulators) can offer a safe learning experience.

Specimens and models are used in conjunction with a variety of instructional methods. They are often used in presenter-paced situations, such as lectures where the actual object can serve as an example to which the learners can refer repeatedly, as various aspects are described. Demonstrations, usually presenter-paced, are done with specimens or models so that the learners can see the procedures or sequence of activities. They are most effective with individuals or small groups. Learner-paced, individual study can effectively include real things or models. Usually accompanied by directions, study guides, or questions, the learner can observe or work for hours until curiosity is satisfied or competency is achieved. In simulation situations, the pacing may be determined by the presenter or the learner, depending on the task. Flight simulators and resuscitation models, for example, attempt to create a realistic, non-threatening experience for the learner. In both of the situations, speed as well as accuracy are crucial, which means that the presenter (the simulator) controls the pace. If the learners respond too slowly, they could lose the patient or the plane. In other simulation situations, where mastery is the critical factor and time unimportant, the pace can be set by the learner.

Specimens and models vary in their potential for interacting with the learner. Inanimate objects tend not to be responsive; however the inanimate simulators just mentioned are computer-based and were developed precisely because they can offer fairly realistic interaction. Animate specimens, such as the microscopic planaria, can provide a full range of realistic interaction.

Overhead transparencies. An overhead transparency is an 8 1/2" x 11" transparent acetate sheet on which words, numbers, charts, graphs, or drawings can be placed. The sheet is placed onto the overhead projector which sends light through the acetate thus projecting words, numbers, etc., onto a screen. It is also possible to use the projector to project silhouettes of three-dimensional objects.

The overhead projector and transparencies are primarily used as part of presenter-paced lectures or discussions. These materials can function in much the same way as a chalkboard. A transparency can be used as an organizer to provide verbal cues, an outline, or a pictorial referent. It can also be used for showing or drawing examples. Some feel that transparencies are static when compared to a chalkboard, because the latter involves the viewer as the presenter writes or draws. Transparencies can be used in the same way; blank spaces can be filled in as the discussion progresses, or important points underlined for emphasis while lecturing. Also, groups involved in discussion during a session or workshop can record their ideas on a transparency and efficiently share the results of their work with the larger group.

The overhead transparency differs from the chalkboard in some noticeable ways. The image is projected and therefore can be made quite large for use with a sizeable audience. Obviously, the size of lettering and drawings must be large enough to be visible to all. Much enlargement can be done by the projector instead of having to make big enough letters on the chalkboard to be seen by a large audience. There is not a space limitation as with the chalkboard, because any number of transparencies can be prepared in advance and used one at a time. With a board, one would have to erase and take the time to produce new information.

Audiotape. Audiotape, on which sound has been recorded, is commonly used to bring such things as music, interviews, speeches, and radio plays into the classroom. As part of a lecture, an audiotape can be presented to a small or large group in order to present information or an example of concepts being presented. Tapes are effective for individual study as well and can be especially useful for recording responses to taped questions or statements. The pace of prerecorded tapes is always determined by the producer of the tape. The music or speech progresses at a certain rate; the presenter or learner can stop and start the tape at various points, but they cannot change the pace of information presentation.

Photographs. The word "photographs" is being used here to indicate pictures which are printed on paper. These kinds of photographs can range in size from the small snapshot to a wall-size print. The most common kinds of photographs used in instruction are pictures from books and magazines, posters, and prints that are individually displayed either on the wall or by the presenter.

Photographs can be used as part of a presenter-paced lecture to a small or moderate size group. They may be displayed temporarily to show an example or left on display throughout the presentation. Singly or in a set, they are also used in learner-paced, individual study, perhaps with a study guide or a set of directing questions. The photos can be studied at length, with the learner selecting the pace and the focus.

Slides. Slides are small, transparent photographs which can be projected onto a screen. Depending on the distance of the projector from the screen, the image can be small or very large. The size of the image is one of the major advantages of slides as compared to photographic prints. The same visual information can be contained in both, but a slide can be used for an audience of 500, while the largest portable photographic print reaches limits of effectiveness with an audience of 30 people. Additionally, the slide format, like an overhead transparency, is often used for displaying limited verbal content, such as verbal cues which can be used to identify and organize upcoming visuals. Brief charts and graphs can be shown, as well as short quotes.

Slides are often used in presenter-paced situations such as lectures. Visual examples can be shown which supplement verbal description. This is a common technique in medical lectures where visual recognition is often essential. Used in this context, the slide image is transient and therefore does not allow for viewer repetition. Slides are also well-suited to individual learner-paced study. Many libraries have carrels that have the equipment necessary to view slides. The learner can study each image for as long as necessary and in any sequence.

Filmstrips. Filmstrips are much like slides in that they present static projected images of pictures and words. They function in the same way as slides and because projected can be used with large groups. They can be a part of a presenter-paced lecture or used in an individual study setting.

A filmstrip, as the name implies, is a strip of film which contains images in an invariant sequence. This lack of flexibility in sequence is a major disadvantage. If you wish to change one image which is out of date or in error, the entire filmstrip must be remade. This format requires a great deal of handling, and being unprotected, the filmstrips are quite vulnerable to scratches, which become distracting lines and spots on the screen.

Slide/filmstrip and audio combinations. Many times, slides and filmstrips have synchronized audio components. This means that the accompanying audiotape or record has audible beeps which tell the presenter to manually advance the visuals, or inaudible beeps which automatically advance the visuals. This technique keeps the auditory information synchronized or coordinated with the appropriate visual information.

These kinds of programs progress at a predetermined pace, the producers having decided how long each visual will remain on the screen, as well as the pace of the auditory track. They can be used as part of a presentation to small and large groups (as the images are projected) or for individual study; however, they do not lend themselves to interactive situations such as class discussion because of the predetermined pace and darkened room. Also it is quite disruptive and distracting for the instructor to attempt to interrupt the presentation to point out important features. For all producer-paced materials, it is recommended that the instructor prepare the group for viewing by indicating what is to be learned or what to look for, and that some follow-up discussion will be held.

Film. Film is similar to slides and filmstrips in that all these media are transparent photographs which are projected onto a screen. Films are often used as part of a lecture, though they may be equally effective when used individually. As with slides and filmstrips, films are uniquely suited to bring the outside world into the instructional setting. They may be made with or without sound, though most do have soundtracks. This is similar to other audio-visual combinations in that the producer determines the visual and audio sequence and the tone and pace of information presentation. The learner must follow along and save up questions for after the show.

Films may be responsive to learners in a limited sense when they include inserted questions, which, after a pause, are answered in some manner.

Film is distinguished from other projected visuals (overheads, slides, filmstrips) in its ability to show motion. Not only can realistic motion be captured, but also slow-motion and time-lapse techniques allow viewers to see things that are imperceptible to the human eye, such as the speeded-up growth of a plant (time lapse) or the contractions of each muscle in a dancer's leg (slow motion).

Videotape. Videotape is not a projected format but is shown on a standard television screen. Videotape is similar to film in many ways: it can show motion and present simultaneous visual and audio information. The only difference between the two is related to the delivery systems. Film is projected, enabling the image to be enlarged onto a screen and therefore shown to a large group. It also must be shown in a darkened room. Video is shown on a television screen, which is relatively small, and therefore is best for small to moderate sized groups, unless several monitors are used.

A videotape is easily stopped, rewound, and advanced, which facilitates viewing or using particular segments of a program.

In addition to showing pretaped programs, a videotape can be used to record the performance of learners (psychomotor skills as well as affective learning). The analysis of the performance and the immediate feedback it provides can be extremely useful in many situations; for example, skiing, tennis, and other sports, interpersonal and non-verbal communication skills, speaking skills, acting, and teaching behavior.

Computerized materials. Computerized materials refer to computer programs with which a learner interacts. They can be learner-paced, or if time is a critical factor in the instruction, such as in certain simulations, they can be program-paced. One of the primary characteristics is responsiveness to the learner, as computerized materials have a great potential for interaction, limited only by the sophistication of the program or the author of the instruction.

Connections can be made between computers and slide projectors or video players. This allows for the display of still or moving images along with the standard text and graphic displays. Connections can also be made with voice synthesizers, which allows for audio presentation of text information.

Matching Methods and Materials to the Instructional Situation

The decision as to which methods and materials should be used for instruction to achieve an objective or set of objectives is an extremely complex one. We usually consider such variables as the size of the group, the physical facilities, the availability of resources and materials, general audience characteristics, such as previous learning, and to some extent, the subject area. In addition, adult educators are informed that they must be facilitators rather than instructors, that adults respond to group interaction and techniques which are relevant to their own experiences, that adults prefer self-directed learning, and that we must never lecture to an audience. However, if all of these "rules" are simultaneously and conscientiously considered, confusing situations arise: how does one handle a large audience expecting an expert presentation at a professional development day; what does one do with a group possessing a wide variety of backgrounds and abilities and expectations; how does one approach a typical college class where one-half or more of the audience are not really adults? It seems next to impossible, short of completely individualized instruction, to match the methods and materials both to the many relevant characteristics of the audience as well as to the nature of the expected learning. It must be accepted that we often cannot offer the ideal methods or materials to all individuals in a group. However, with careful planning, with options, variety, and flexibility, we can hope to select strategies which are more appropriate than if these variables are not considered at all.

In order to simplify the process, selection of instructional strategies will be discussed in relation to three criteria:

1. *objectives*, including the level and domain of learning and the requirements of the task;

2. *audience characteristics*; and

3. *constraints* of the instructional situation.

Considering the Objectives

It is clear that the nature of the expected learning determines, in part, the instructional approach. Learning to swim by attending a lecture on swimming is not likely to be effective. The domain and level of learning and the requirements of the task (e.g. verbal or written response) should be considered.

Domain and level of learning. The matrix provided in Table 5-4 provides some suggestions as to appropriate methods for each of the levels in the three domains of learning. These suggestions must not be considered as "absolute" rules: the other characteristics of the situation must be

TABLE 5–4: Matching Methods to Domain and Level of Learning

DOMAIN & LEVEL OF LEARNING	MOST APPROPRIATE METHODS
COGNITIVE DOMAIN	
KNOWLEDGE	Lecture, Programmed Instruction, Drill and Practice
COMPREHENSION	Lecture, Modularized Instruction, Programmed Instruction
APPLICATION	Discussion, Simulations and Games, CAI, Modularized Instruction, Field Experience, Laboratory
ANALYSIS	Discussion, Independent/Group Projects, Simulations, Field Experience, Role-Playing, Laboratory
SYNTHESIS	Independent/Group Projects, Field Experience, Role-Playing, Laboratory
EVALUATION	Independent/Group Projects, Field Experience, Laboratory
AFFECTIVE DOMAIN	
RECEIVING	Lecture, Discussion, Modularized Instruction, Field Experience
RESPONDING	Discussion, Simulations, Modularized Instruction, Role-Playing, Field Experience
VALUING	Discussion, Independent/Group Projects, Simulations, Role-Playing, Field Experience
ORGANIZATION	Discussion, Independent/Group Projects, Field Experience
CHARACTERIZATION BY A VALUE	Independent Projects, Field Experience
PSYCHOMOTOR DOMAIN	
PERCEPTION	Demonstration (lecture), Drill and Practice
SET	Demonstration (lecture), Drill and Practice
GUIDED RESPONSE	Peer Teaching, Games, Role-Playing, Field Experience, Drill and Practice
MECHANISM	Games, Role-Playing, Field Experience, Drill and Practice
COMPLEX OVERT RESPONSE	Games, Field Experience
ADAPTATION	Independent Projects, Games, Field Experience
ORIGINATION	Independent Projects, Games, Field Experience

considered as well. However, here we have an important starting point to selecting appropriate strategies.

At the lower levels of the cognitive domain (knowledge and comprehension) and at the receiving level of the affective domain, the goal of the instruction is to expose learners to information, concepts, or values. Learners are only expected to demonstrate that they have received and retained the information—they do not "use" it in any other way. The instructor-centered methods, such as the lecture, and the less interactive materials, such as oral presentation, texts, or films, are efficient in conveying information. This is not to say that knowledge or comprehension learning does not occur with interactive methods or materials (some educators advocate these strategies for all types of learning), but the lecture or the textbook are both effective and efficient and should not be dismissed because we are dealing with adult learners.

At the application and analysis levels of the cognitive domain and at the responding and valuing levels of the affective domain, learners should be more actively involved with the content of the instruction. They are using the information in new situations and developing their own attitudes or values. The nature of this type of learning requires that learners interact with the concepts in some way, or that they interact with their peers or the instructor or with other individuals in the real situation. The most appropriate methods and materials are those which provide for this interaction, involvement, or participation. Participants can learn by discussions, simulations, and games, interaction with modules or computer assisted instruction, or involvement in the field. The appropriate materials still include oral presentation and audio or visual presentations (but in conjunction with an interactive method), and depending on the subject area, specimens or models may be important materials for facilitating the necessary participation.

At the highest levels of the cognitive and affective domains (synthesis, evaluation, organization, characterization by a value), more complex behaviors are expected, usually with less instructor guidance. Learners are writing essays, developing plans or projects or products, judging the quality of others' performances, and developing value systems. In order to develop these skills or values, the learner must be actively involved in situations in which they are used. Independent or group projects with feedback from the instructor are valuable. In some subject areas, field experience is essential, and often role-playing or laboratory work is important. As can be seen from this selection of methods, the learners are given the opportunity to *do* what they are expected to learn. The accompanying materials would be dependent on the subject: oral materials, in the form of discussions are useful in integrating the results of experiences; specimens (interaction with the real thing) are often important, and texts or audio and visual materials may provide the information with which the learner works. At these levels, the materials are closely integrated with the methods and are rarely in themselves the vehicle for instruction as they can be at the lower levels.

Learning in the psychomotor domain requires a different type of involvement—physical practice of the skill being taught. It is very unlikely that anyone could learn to ski or pronounce words in a second language or administer an injection by reading about the procedure (in spite of the proliferation of books about skiing and tennis). Some oral presentation, however, is usually required, and exposure to a demonstration of a skill (through audio or visual materials or with a human "model") can often be useful. The use of these materials must be followed by the opportunity for the learner to attempt the skill and receive feedback on the accuracy of the performance. At the lower levels of the psychomotor domain, the methods could include games, role-playing, field experience, drill and practice, and, possibly, peer teaching. The accompanying materials would vary depending on the skill being taught, but oral presentation (feedback from instructor or peers), slides or film (to demonstrate procedures), videotapes (to either demonstrate or to provide feedback), and specimens (the props or equipment used) are likely to be a part of the instructional process. At the higher levels of the psychomotor domain (complex overt response, adaptation, and origination), games and field experience become the predominant methods. For adaptation and origination, depending on the subject areas, independent projects may also be important (e.g. the development of a dance routine). The materials used with these methods could consist of oral presentation (feedback from instructor or peers), videotapes (usually for feedback), and specimens (equipment).

Requirements of the task. When matching methods and materials to objectives, it is necessary to consider the requirements of the learning task. It would be possible, for example, to have various objectives at the knowledge level of the cognitive domain, such as "discriminate among and identify bird calls" or "discriminate among and identify spices," which would require quite different instructional approaches.

The learners required to "discriminate among and identify bird calls" should be provided with auditory stimuli, such as live sound, audio taped sound, video with audio track, slides with audio, film or filmstrip with audio. Materials with a visual component should only be selected if the visual stimuli support and do not distract from the learning task. In addition, a symbolic component would be necessary to allow the learner to relate the auditory stimuli to the appropriate verbal (written or spoken) label. The learner required to "discriminate among and identify spices" should be provided with actual spices that can be smelled and tasted in order to allow for recognition and discrimination. In addition, a verbal (symbolic) component must be included in the instruction.

Table 5-2 (Delivery System and Form of Twelve Common Instructional Materials) may be a useful reference when considering requirements of the task: it provides information about the form (concrete to abstract) and sensory stimuli provided by various common instructional materials.

Psychomotor learning is usually an observable behavior, (e.g. playing the piano or swimming). The requirements of the task usually demand the performance of physical skills, which means that the learner must practice the required actions in order to become proficient. The instruction, methods, and materials selected must include opportunity to perform the activity, perhaps repeatedly. If the objective is, "the learner will perform the piano piece, *Für Elise,*" then the method selected must be experiential, playing the piece, and the materials selected must be the piano (the real thing), and the music (symbolic).

Cognitive learning can only be inferred by observing a behavior. The concern is not whether the learner can physically manipulate the pencil to write words on paper, but whether the words that are written down indicate comprehension of a concept. The learner must have practice in thinking, which means that the methods and materials selected must facilitate the required cognitive process.

Objectives including outcomes such as "describe," "define," or "list" could require written or oral verbal response. In all cases verbal outcomes are implied, which means that the learner must be allowed to practice written or oral responses.

If the objectives indicate that the learner will "recognize" or "identify," there is an implied visual perceptual requirement. The learner may be required to recognize words, in which case an appropriate learning experience could be provided by written text, words on overhead transparency, words on slides, words on the chalkboard, or words on a computer terminal. The learner may be required to recognize pictures, in which case appropriate learning stimuli could be provided by photographs, slides, filmstrip, videotape, film, etc. The participants may be required to recognize the "real thing" in which case, depending on the nature of the actual object (size, proximity), stimuli could be provided in the form of a picture in various formats, models, or the real thing. The nature of the response indicates which material should be selected for instruction in order to allow learners to practice appropriate behaviors.

At the higher levels of the cognitive domain, more input and processing are necessary to achieve the final task or objective. For this reason, as many more possibilities exist for methods and materials, the selection depends on what the learner will be *doing*.

Affective learning, the internal change in attitudes or values, also only can be inferred by observing an external behavior. Since the learning is internal, we can only observe ostensible evidence of learning. Methods and materials may not be directly related to the required task. They are aimed towards influencing predispositions. Objectives, however, are stated in observable behaviors that may be the result of a particular predisposition. For example, the objective might be, "the learner will voluntarily purchase lift tickets and ski one day each week." The concern is not whether the learner physically can ski, but whether he or she is interested in and willing to try skiing. We are not primarily concerned with providing practice in skiing; what we need to provide are some positive experiences that will encourage the learner to ski or to attempt skiing. An appropriate approach would be to provide positive role models, such as people who also seem to be enjoying themselves at the activity. This could be done by watching a film or watching and talking to real people. There may not be an apparent match, for the affective domain, between requirement of the task, objectives, and materials. The task may require an apparent cognitive or psychomotor behavior, but in order to change the attitude, the instructional materials must be directed at the attitude or value system—not the cognitive or psychomotor behavior.

Table 5-5 may help to clarify this discussion. Various objectives of different domains and levels are listed. For each, requirements of the task and examples of appropriate instructional materials are given. It is important to note the relation among the three columns. The requirement of the task, or what the learner must do to be successful, is derived from the objective. The appropriate materials to use in instruction must allow the learner to become involved in the activity that ultimately will be required.

When selecting appropriate materials for the requirements of the task, the instructor must consider the form (concrete to abstract) of the instruction as well as the sensory stimulation necessary. Reference to Table 5-2 is recommended, as it includes much of this information for various instructional materials.

Summary. The matching of methods and materials to the objectives is primarily concerned with providing the learner with an opportunity to be involved in the type of activity or process which is expected to be a product of the instruction. The methods and materials, therefore, which are chosen for the recall of names or dates must be quite different than those chosen for the development of professional ethics or for physical skills.

TABLE 5–5: Selection of Materials Based on Requirements of the Task

OBJECTIVE	REQUIREMENTS OF THE TASK	EXAMPLES OF APPROPRIATE INSTRUCTIONAL MATERIALS
The student will be able to label the parts of the ear when a drawing is provided	- visual recognition (of drawing) and - written verbal response (labelling)	*Form*: Illusions & Symbols *Examples*: a) color or black & white drawing with written labels b) overhead transparency with written labels supplemented with spoken terms c) drawing on chalkboard with written labels
The student will be able to explain the procedure for performing a binary search for a name in a telephone directory	- written verbal response and/or - oral verbal response	A. *Form*: Symbols *Examples*: a) written verbal descriptions b) oral verbal descriptions B. *Form*: Illusion & Symbols *Examples*: a) diagram of procedure accompanied by written or oral verbal description
The student will be able to prepare a presentation to be given to the class on the effect of the defeat of the Equal Rights Amendment on the status of women	Requirement not clearly defined Presentation could have various formats. E.g.: - oral verbal presentation - oral verbal presentation with written words on chalkboard, overhead or handout - slide-tape presentation including images, with oral and/or written verbal portions	A. *Form*: Symbols *Examples*: a) written materials (articles, books) b) oral verbal materials (e.g., interviews, tapes of speeches, radio news programs) B. *Form*: Illusion & Symbols *Examples*: Images and spoken/written words which describe and/or show effects of E.R.A. a) television news b) film c) text with photographs

TABLE 5–5: Selection of Materials Based on Requirements of the Task (continued)

OBJECTIVE	REQUIREMENTS OF THE TASK	EXAMPLES OF APPROPRIATE INSTRUCTIONAL MATERIALS
After completion of a course in downhill skiing, the student voluntarily purchases lift tickets and skis at least one day per week	- voluntary action that demonstrates interest and motivation	A. *Form*: Real Things *Examples*: a) observing and interacting verbally and non-verbally with role models who are enjoying the activity B. *Form*: Illusions & Symbols *Examples*: Images and spoken/written words of people enjoying the activity a) film b) video tape
The student will make a commitment to a career in.... *(any number of fields could be inserted here; e.g., music, social work, chemistry)*	- motivation to pursue career - persistence - valuing importance of work	*Form*: Real Things *Examples*: a) Interact with professionals in professional environment and *Form*: Symbols *Examples*: a) Inspiring book: e.g., biography/autobiography of professional and *Form*: Illusion & Symbols *Examples*: Images and words (spoken or written) depicting/describing life experiences of various successful professionals. E.g.: a) film b) television program c) slide-tape

TABLE 5–5: Selection of Materials Based on Requirements of the Task (continued)

OBJECTIVE	REQUIREMENTS OF THE TASK	EXAMPLES OF APPROPRIATE INSTRUCTIONAL MATERIALS
The student will be able to create a modern dance routine based on previously learned steps and sub-routines	- visualization of a three-dimensional movement within a defined space - integrating actions in unique combinations - performing actions (physical skills are not necessarily required, however, as the emphasis is on "create")	A. *Form*: Illusion & Symbols *Examples*: a) documentary film of process of creating a dance routine (instructs in process) B. *Form*: Real Thing *Examples*: a) attending various modern dance performances (instructs in product)
The student will be able to prepare a white wine sauce by following a recipe	- read and interpret recipe (written symbols) - perform actions required by recipe	A. *Form*: Real Things & Symbols *Examples*: a) demonstrate the actual procedure giving oral verbal and/or written verbal description/instructions b) student performs the procedure following verbal instructions B. *Form*: Illusion & Symbols *Examples*: a) videotaped demonstration of procedure accompanied by oral and/or written verbal description/instructions

Considering the Audience

In Chapter Two, audience characteristics were described and entry behaviors discussed. As mentioned, the consideration of these variables can quickly seem to be overwhelming, as each member of the audience probably has a different combination of learning style, experience, self-esteem, anxiety, ability, and so on. In practice, "considering the audience" usually means: (a) being *aware* of audience characteristics and their possible effect; (b) considering the general characteristics of the adult learner and accepting that every adult is not a typical "adult learner"; (c) providing a variety of methods and materials that are appropriate to the expected learning; and (d) being flexible, providing options, and being willing to change tactics when things are not working. It will not be possible to provide the ideal strategy for every individual in an audience. It has been argued that this is neither necessary, nor even an effective or efficient approach to instruction as most learners *can* learn using techniques that are not their preferred techniques. Perhaps the best we can hope to do is to provide some activities in any one session that match the preferred style of some of the audience, and in general, to match up with the background and level and experience of the group as a whole.

This sounds like a pessimistic view of teaching—we'll never manage to do it right! However, the instructor of adults will find that it does make a difference in interest, motivation, and learning when every effort is made to match the strategies to the needs of the audience. This process will be discussed in four parts: facilitating learning for adults, considering the level of instruction, considering experience and prior knowledge, and special needs. Personality variables and preferred learning style are excluded from the discussion, since any one audience is likely to have a variety of personality characteristics and all preferred learning styles; the only answer to this is to provide a variety of strategies whenever possible. Fuhrmann and Grasha (1983) provide an excellent summary of appropriate instructional strategies for the various learning styles.

Adult learners. Some of the general characteristics of adults as learners were summarized in Chapter Two. The implications of these characteristics for the selection of methods and materials will be discussed. Brundage and Mackeracher (1980) provide a much more extensive list of characteristics, with each described in terms of its implications for program planning. The reader is referred to this excellent and comprehensive summary of adult audience characteristics for further detail. Other detailed discussions of the adult learner are provided by Cross (1980), Knowles (1980), Darkenwald and Miriam (1983), and Brookfield (1986). For the instructor, however, who is planning a workshop, course, or other specific instructional situation, it is not practical to consider and act upon as many as 36 learning principles (Brundage and Mackeracher, 1980).

The adult learner has usually chosen to attend the instructional situation and therefore has clear and specific goals. It is essential that these goals be identified and addressed, or the audience will quickly lose attention and interest. This implies that, regardless of group size, time constraints, or any other variable, some form of discussion must take place in which the audience has the opportunity to express their goals. At times, this may be done in advance, such as during registration for a workshop or orientation sessions for a course or program. But even if the instructor is facing an unknown group for a two-hour session, time must be taken to ask, "what do you want to know?" and then this information must be acted upon. An interactive strategy is clearly required to deal with this audience characteristic appropriately.

Adult learners have a variety of experiences, and learning is facilitated when the instruction is related to these experiences. Again, an interactive approach is required: the nature of the relevant experiences must be determined and acted upon. This can involve discussion during instruction or the collecting of information prior to instruction.

Most adults have immediate goals. They wish to learn a specific skill or have a specific need addressed. Interaction is required to determine the nature of the goals of the audience, if this is not apparent from the fact that they attended a particular session. Usually, "immediate" goals implies that the learner wishes to be able to *do* something and that the learning be practical. The strategies then must allow for the *doing*, interactive or experiential, depending on the subject area.

Usually adults prefer to be self-directed learners. They prefer having input into the instructional situation and working on tasks that are relevant to their needs, at their own pace, without being told what to do. The instructional methods should be interactive in order to obtain the input. Individualized instruction best meets the needs of an audience who wish to work on their own tasks at their own pace. When this is not practical, optional activities and independent or group projects will facilitate self-directed learning. The use of appropriate evaluation techniques (Chapter Six) is also crucial here.

If the audience includes older adult learners, their physical requirements must be considered, particularly in terms of instructional materials and physical facilities. Print on the chalkboard or overhead transparency should be large and clear; volume should be appropriate on any audio materials. Lighting should be bright and furniture comfortable. When selecting methods, whether or not any learner wears a hearing aid should be considered, as that individual will not be able to focus on any one conversation if numerous group discussions are taking place in the room.

Adults have established opinions, values, and behaviors which must be respected. Again, an interactive approach is essential to ascertain what those opinions, values, and behaviors are. If they conflict with expected learning, we are dealing with affective learning or change and should treat the process accordingly.

Although an adult may have a positive self-concept in his or her own life, when returning to a learning situation, there may be extensive anxiety and self-doubt. It is important that the learner experience success and be encouraged and rewarded in the learning activity. This usually implies an interactive instructional strategy, either with instructor or with peers, in which on-going positive feedback is provided. Consideration of the appropriate level of instruction is essential.

Level. The level of instruction clearly affects the selection of methods and materials to some extent. This is, of course, confounded with other variables, such as previous learning in the area, intellectual development, and the domain and level of learning. However, quite generally, in an introductory session in an area, the method is more likely to be instructor-centered and in advanced sessions, either independent or experiential.

The level of instruction also must take into account the newness of the learner to the instructional situation. An introductory workshop on word processing, for example, will probably attract secretarial staff who have not previously attended such sessions. They will be anxious and concerned about their ability to perform. Some of the general characteristics of the adult learner must be disregarded; guidance and support will be required, not self-directed learning.

Experience or prior knowledge. A learner's previous experience with a topic has often been cited as an essential consideration in the selection of materials. Dale's (1969) Cone of Experience (Figure 5-2) indicates that as we move from very concrete learning materials (real things) to very abstract materials (symbols, such as words spoken and written) the potential for providing experience becomes increasingly limited. Hence, direct purposeful activity is placed at the broad base of the cone, indicating a large potential for providing experience, and verbal symbols are placed at the apex of the cone, indicating limited experiential potential. Adjacent to Dale's Cone of Experience is Torkelson's (1975) Concept Cone (Figure 5-2), which is wide at the top and pointed at the bottom. The distinction between cones is that Torkelson's is concerned with the amount of experience the learner has with a concept, as opposed to the amount of experience that one can gain from a particular learning experience. A learner

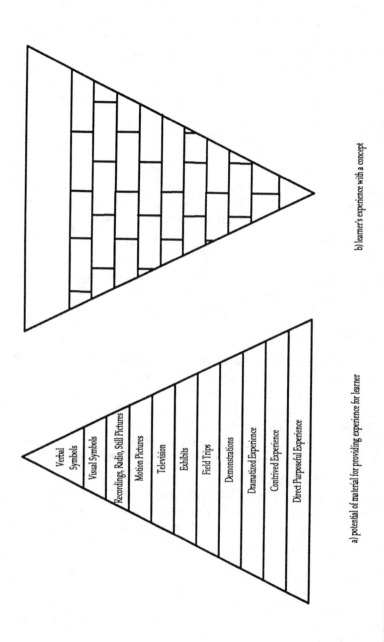

a) potential of material for providing experience for learner

b) learner's experience with a concept

Figure 5–2: (a) Dale's Cone of Experience and (b) Torkelson's Concept Cone

may have a great deal of experience with one concept (wide top) and little experience with another concept (pointed bottom). This suggests that when a learner has much experience with a concept, it is appropriate to use symbolic forms of instruction. The learner already familiar with a concept can manipulate related ideas and therefore should be able to work on an abstract level. For the learner who has little or no experience with a concept, instruction will be more successful if it occurs at a more concrete level. Concrete materials (e.g. real things, models) allow learners to experience the full range of attributes associated with an object, process, or procedure.

In general, instruction should provide materials that fit the learner's previous experience or prior knowledge of a concept. It is often suggested that instruction which begins at more concrete levels be followed by activities that require the learner to manipulate symbols (e.g. a follow-up discussion or essay). This will facilitate the development of the learner's ability to work with symbols.

Special needs. Sometimes a group will include a learner or learners who have special perceptual or physical characteristics which affect the selection of methods and materials. Language, visual, auditory, or physical handicaps may be present. The special needs of the older adult were described in Chapter Two. The instructor should be cognizant of these needs and design appropriate learning experiences which will accommodate individuals when necessary. Reading materials, for example, must be selected with care when people are learning in their second language, and the instructor may consider presenting concepts through more than one form (e.g. symbols and illusion). A visually impaired learner would obviously lead the instructor to provide alternative (e.g. audio) materials; the presence of an individual in a wheelchair would limit the extensive use of active games or simulations.

The adaptation of instructional methods and materials to special needs is a topic which has received extensive attention in the literature and can only be mentioned briefly here. The instructional designer who is considering a special audience should refer to this literature.

Considering Constraints of the Instructional Situation

Several characteristics of the instructional situation, in addition to the audience and the type of learning, should be considered in the selection of instructional strategies:

1. group size
2. required or voluntary learning
3. physical facilities

4. resources

5. time of day

6. instructor preference or expertise

Table 5-3 may be a useful reference when considering constraints of the instructional situation, as it includes information regarding the optimal group size, facilities, and expertise required for various common media.

Group size usually only directly affects the choice of teaching methods when the group is quite large. When the group contains more than about 30 individuals, discussions begin to lose their effectiveness, and sizes of over 40 prevent the use of large group discussions. Nearly all of the experiential learning methods become impossible in large groups unless several assistants are available, and the individualized learning methods quickly become a management nightmare. Usually, large groups exist only at the introductory levels in higher education or in one-time presentations, such as professional development days. In these cases, the instructor-centered methods are probably appropriate. Independent learning can be used, particularly if assistance is available for tutoring and feedback.

The adult educator, though, shouldn't be completely discouraged at facing a group of 60 or 100 individuals for a particular session. With careful management, strategies other than the lecture can be used if they are appropriate for the nature of the expected learning. Although every situation is different, the following example might illustrate the process and give courage to the new adult educator. The setting is a professional development day for college instructors. The topic is evaluation of teaching. The audience consists of 120 instructors, most of whom have a few years of teaching experience. A lecture, then, is not particularly appropriate, since each individual in the audience will already have his or her own ideas and experiences with evaluation. First, the room is arranged so that people are sitting in 12 groups of 10 individuals each. The topic is briefly presented and broken down into a series of steps. For each step, a brief exercise has been prepared for group discussion. Since individuals are already in groups, there is no shuffling of tables and chairs. The 12 groups go through each of the exercises; after each exercise, one group (or two, depending on time) presents their results to the large group. The leader of this session introduces and summarizes each step. Most of the activity is interactive, yet very focussed and structured and carefully timed. This is more difficult but probably more effective than an instructor-centered lecture on the topic. People are busy, talking to each other, thinking about the topic, using their experiences, relating new ideas to what they already know.

Whether the instruction is *required or voluntary* is likely to affect learner interest and motivation, which in turn affects the selection of strategies. Individuals who have been "forced" to attend a professional development workshop may be thinking about just getting through the day; a person who has chosen a course or workshop undoubtedly has immediate personal or professional goals and will be interested in pursuing independent projects, using modularized instruction, talking with peers, and so on. In some cases, required instruction will result in learners with a high achievement motivation, as they know they must do well in order to maintain their career goals. These learners will be interested in efficient communication of material by an expert (instructor-centered methods).

Wherever it is practical, the adult educator should find out why the participants are there. Those who are required to attend will probably prefer efficient strategies with an expert or formal authority instructor style; those who have chosen to attend will probably wish to pursue their own interests, goals, and projects. It can be dangerous to generalize in this way; individual learners will react in different ways regardless of the situation, but instructor awareness of this variable is valuable.

The *physical facilities* of the room or institution can affect the choice of instructional strategies. If, for example, there are few facilities for independent research (library resources, a quiet working environment), then the independent learning methods will be less effective. If the room does not have moveable chairs and tables, it is difficult to organize group discussions. At times, the shape of the room (e.g. a wide, shallow room) will prevent effective use of visual media such as chalkboards, slides, or videotapes. It is essential for the instructor, prior to the selection of methods and materials, to inspect the physical facilities available for instruction.

Other institutional *resources* clearly affect the choice of methods and materials. For example, if no facilities exist for the production of audio or visual media, these techniques cannot be easily used unless the instructor or the institution is willing to purchase commercially prepared materials. At times, even the basic audio-visual equipment is not available. Similarly, restrictions on copying might hamper the development and use of modularized instruction, and a restricted materials budget will influence the use of programmed instruction, optional textbooks, etc. A lack of or limited computer facilities will affect the decision to use computerized instruction. If the group size is large and assistants are not available, the instructor will be understandably reluctant to use methods which require a great deal of individual interaction with the learners.

Time and money often strongly influence the choice of instructional strategies. Instructors often lack the time to create appropriate activities or locate resources. With budget restraint, resources such as audio-visual materials may simply not be available.

Given these constraints, the responsibility lies with the instructor to be creative in the use of the basic methods and inexpensive, readily available materials. The chalkboard, newspapers, and other everyday materials can be inexpensively used in many cases.

Although it is difficult to generalize across subject areas and levels of instruction, the *time of day* that the instruction is offered may be a consideration in the selection of methods and materials. In an evening or late afternoon session, particularly when individuals are arriving after a day's work, both methods and materials should contain changes of pace, variety in methods, more interaction, more active involvement, and probably more humour and "drama." Weary learners, who are faced with extensive use of the lecture method, may not be as likely to retain the given information as when they are actively involved.

Both learners and instructors have preferred times of day, times when they feel most mentally alert. If the instructor or a large number of the participants seem to be at their low point, method and material selection may need to be modified again so as to step up the pace—more variety, active involvement, discussion, role playing, games.

For full-time students at the college or university level, the nature of the class immediately preceding or following the session may also be a consideration in planning the activities. Learners who have arrived in a required history class after leaving their favorite physical education class face an abrupt change in environment. Perhaps, dependent on the schedule, the initial method used can be chosen so as either to subdue the eager discussion of sports or to stimulate interest and involvement for those who have just left a passive lecture-method course.

In practice, the selection of methods and materials for instruction is often based more on *instructor preference and expertise* than on any other factor mentioned so far. The teacher who has good public speaking ability and has lectured for years may tend to gravitate towards the instructor-centered methods which are most comfortable and familiar. The instructor who is uncertain about particular procedures will avoid demonstration. The natural, energetic organizer may tend to create interactive instructional situations. The teacher who learns best from experience will often provide experiential instruction. The same can be said in terms of materials selected. The instructor who has atrocious handwriting may avoid using the chalkboard, while others may prefer this familiar mode of instructional support. Instructors who have never operated a slide-tape equipment combination often avoid using materials that require such equipment, for fear of appearing inept in front of the group. Very often, appropriate instructional materials, perhaps real things or models for demonstrations or films, are not available. To incorporate such materials into instruction would require that the instructor create or produce the necessary materials. Most individuals do not have the skills necessary to produce such materials, much less the time or money to invest in the effort. Therefore the most appropriate materials may not be used due to instructor preference or expertise.

While we should have as a goal the selection and use of methods and materials that are as appropriate as possible for the given instructional situation, practical constraints such as instructor preference will have an impact on the decision. Undoubtedly an instructor will perform more effectively when using preferred methods and materials, and this is an important consideration. An overall strategy to improve the variety of methods and materials used is to incorporate only one new technique at a time and only when the instructor is familiar and comfortable with the methods, materials, and context of the rest of the session. Often the participants are a great help in a new situation. If the instructor has never used an overhead transparency, for example, he or she might ask working groups to record their ideas on transparencies, then share those ideas with the large group by using the overhead projector. Not only is this an effective strategy for communicating ideas, but it will increase the instructor's comfort with the medium. Also, there is nothing at all wrong in saying to your group that you are trying a method for the first time—in fact, it often helps to build rapport with your audience! Participants are usually helpful and supportive in such a situation, while the instructor gains confidence in the new method.

Summary

Instructional methods have been described under four headings: instructor-centered, interactive, individualized, and experiential. Each method in these categories was seen to have its own distinguishing characteristics, some of which are either advantages or disadvantages depending on the instructional situation. Instructional materials, the resources used to present stimuli to the learner, were described in terms of the delivery system (e.g. transparencies, slides) and the form or condition of abstraction (e.g. real things, symbols, illusions). Again, distinguishing features of the materials and their advantages and disadvantages were presented. Finally, the complex process of selecting the appropriate methods and materials for a particular instructional situation was analyzed. These decisions must be based on the nature of the expected learning (the domain and level), the characteristics of the audience, and the practical constraints of the instructional setting.

The multitude of variables discussed and the complex interactions among them may tend to leave the instructor feeling that there can be no solution, possibly no "good" instruction. Often as teachers we really just want to know if we should use examples, or films, or encourage discussion. Although it is clear that straightforward answers rarely exist, it is possible to describe some general principles of effective instruction. The final section of this chapter will address that issue.

General Characteristics of Effective Instruction

This chapter has discussed the complex process of selecting the most appropriate instructional materials and methods. Yet when the strategies for a session are being planned, one also looks for general good teaching ideas. Even though the research and practical guidelines indicate that there is no *one* best approach, there are some established general characteristics of effective instruction.

A considerable amount of research has been conducted on the psychology of learning; this is an area far too broad to be summarized here. Unfortunately, less work has been done on the process of adult learning, but a good summary is provided by Brookfield (1986). From such investigations, there are some accepted principles of learning that can be applied to the design of any instructional strategy, regardless of methods or materials that are most appropriate for a specific situation.

Instructor Awareness of the Audience

As was discussed in Chapter Two, it is essential that the instructor be aware of various characteristics of the audience when instruction is planned. In particular, it is important in the design of any effective instruction, that learners' prerequisite skills be either formally or informally assessed. To take some extreme examples, one cannot expect learners to solve algebraic problems when the basic arithmetic skills have not been mastered, and one cannot expect the production of clear, well-organized written work when individuals have not mastered grammar or spelling. The use of a hierarchical instructional analysis (Chapter Four) indicates what a learner must be able to do before beginning a specific objective; at some point the instructor will choose to regard a skill or a concept as a prerequisite, and it is this expectation which must be evaluated.

Learner Awareness of What is Expected

In Chapter Two the value of objectives to facilitate learning and the planning of feedback or evaluation techniques was stressed. This holds true whether the objectives are designed solely by the instructor, in collaboration with the learners, or solely by the learners. Everyone has to know what is going to happen. It has been shown in the research literature that learners' performance improves when they have some way of "orienting" themselves (objectives, advance organizers, etc.). Common sense tells us, as well, that we are not likely to learn efficiently when we don't know what we're trying to learn. The frustration of such an experience can lead participants to memorize irrelevant details and to attempt to outguess the instructor. (Remember the coffee break conversations debating "what she really wants us to do".) Since our ultimate goal as instructors is to have the learners leave the session with a certain body of knowledge or set of skills, it is reasonable to discuss and negotiate these expectations with the audience. Regardless of the instructional strategy employed, this will be a characteristic of effective instruction.

Feedback

It is essential that learners receive feedback on their progress in meeting the expectations set for the instructional situation. In general, frequent, immediate, and specific feedback is needed to facilitate learning; however in some situations, such as with very large groups or very advanced or independent learners, this may not always be practical. Frequent feedback allows learners to keep track of their progress and to avoid wasting time on irrelevant learning or in practising bad habits. Feedback which follows quickly after a performance provides stronger reinforcement and also better serves to discourage errors or incorrect procedures. Receiving the results of a test weeks after it has been written no longer provides the learner with useful information. Specific feedback allows the learner to focus on the aspects of the learning process which need improvement. There's no point in saying, "that wasn't so good" when the learner finishes changing a tire. Instead, point out what she did wrong and how she can improve. Similarly, there's not much purpose in writing "good" on an independent project: what, specifically, were the strengths of the work?

Feedback should, of course, be given informally throughout any instructional situation (in addition to, or often rather than grading or testing). Through discussions, questions, responses to questions, comments, and non-verbal communication (smiling, nodding, body posture) the instructor is continually providing on-going, immediate, and specific feedback to the learner.

Feedback to the Instructor

As important as feedback to the learner is feedback to the instructor regarding his or her effectiveness. The instructor is a learner as well and needs feedback on performance. This can be done in several ways; details on techniques for obtaining feedback from the audience are described in Chapter Seven. Questionnaires, interviews, or discussions can be used to determine learners' perceptions of the instructional effectiveness. More informally, feedback can be obtained through anecdotal records, comments, questions, and casual interaction with the participants.

Active Learner Involvement

Regardless of the instructional methods and materials selected, it is important to incorporate active learner involvement into the teaching and learning process. Individuals who listen passively to a lecture without answering or asking questions, discussing issues, or applying skills after the session are less likely to retain the information. In some areas of learning, such as the psychomotor domain, this principle is obvious—we realize that "learning by doing" is essential. However, in any domain or at any level, some active participation will facilitate learning. Interest and motivation are stimulated, and feedback is provided directly or indirectly through most forms of participation. The type of involvement will vary dependent on the instructional situation, but may include questioning, inviting questions, discussion among participants, group exercises, simulations, field applications, projects, and presentations by participants.

Examples and Illustrations

Learning is facilitated by the provision of concrete examples and illustrations through which the individual can relate the new information to his or her own experience. Research on learning shows us that learning takes place when the individual can associate new material with familiar or previously learned information, or when the individual can classify the new information with the familiar. Examples, illustrations, or clear statements that point out relationships to the audience's previous experiences will facilitate the learning process. In a psychology course, for example, the concept of "positive reinforcement" will be more easily understood when the audience observes an illustration such as a cat ringing a bell to obtain food. In an introductory nursing course, the general concept of safety will become more concrete if the instructor describes examples of safe and unsafe nursing behaviors. The adult learner usually enjoys providing examples from his or her own experience which can be related to the new information. Group exercises which involve the generation of examples, applications, illustrations, and implications help the learners to connect the new to the old.

Examples and illustrations take many forms—real things, symbols, illusions—and can be part of any teaching method.

Organization

Another essential component of effective instruction is an organization or structure which: (a) follows the sequence produced by an instructional analysis (Chapter Four); (b) provides relationships among topics; (c) distinguishes among major and minor topics; and (d) provides frequent, cumulative review. We have all probably read a poorly structured novel or listened to a rambling, unorganized talk. It becomes increasingly difficult to absorb the information in such a delivery, and we usually experience anxiety, frustration, or boredom. The situation is the same with any type of instruction: a lecture, a discussion, a textbook, or a filmstrip. This need for structure may seem to contradict the principle of self-directed learning and/or learner input into the instructional process; however, regardless of the way in which the instruction is planned, a clear organization must be achieved. A situation in which all participants are struggling to be heard and where there is no clearly agreed-upon goal to the activity will not be effective even though everyone may have input into it. Flaws in sequencing may lead to learners trying to learn skills for which they do not have the prerequisites. Without stated connections among topics, individuals may resort to fragmented memorization of material and a lack of distinction between topics. Cumulative review provides reinforcement of what has been learned and allows learner self-evaluation.

Flexibility

The teaching and learning process is a complex interaction between the learner, the instructor, and the variables in the environment. Effective instruction must be adaptive to unexpected or unknown characteristics of the situation. This adaptability can be as simple as the willingness to repeat or rephrase an explanation or as complex as the redesign of a segment of instruction, based on the needs of a particular group. Flexibility facilitates learning by better meeting the needs of the audience. There are often characteristics of the audience that we are not aware of until instruction is in progress. When this occurs, it remains a priority to consider the needs of the learner, and thus it is important to adapt to unforseen needs. It sounds frightening, but once again, there's nothing wrong with saying, "I see this isn't working, let's reconsider the way we're doing this." The audience will respect and work better with the instructor who stops and adjusts than with the individual who forges ahead regardless of the consequences, simply because the session has been planned that way.

Summary

Several general characteristics of effective instruction have been listed and briefly discussed. This list is not intended to be complete; indeed, theorists and researchers in education admit that they cannot thoroughly describe good teaching. The complexity of the teaching and learning process presents many research problems. However, we are aware, to a limited extent, of strategies that facilitate learning for most individuals, and these strategies should be incorporated into all instructional methods and materials.

CHAPTER SIX

EVALUATING LEARNING

Evaluation of learning is a necessary component of every teaching and learning situation. "Learning" is defined as any change in knowledge, skill, or value system, and change can only be judged by some assessment or evaluation. The term "evaluation" will be used to include a wide array of activities, such as informal observation of audience reactions, tests, structured observations of performance, and the use of discussions and anecdotal records or comments to provide feedback to the learner. The systematic design of instruction includes a consideration of the approach or philosophy of the evaluation, a selection of evaluation techniques, matching the evaluation procedures to the instructional situation and the characteristics of the audience, and the construction of evaluation instruments.

The choice between formal and informal evaluation procedures is related to the educational system in which one is working. Professional development workshops, in-service seminars, and general interest sessions rarely include formal evaluation of learning. Knowles (1980) argues that the adult educator should not formally assess learning, but rather that learner self-evaluation should be encouraged and facilitated. In many situations, this would be the preferred approach to evaluation. A great deal of adult education, however, takes place within systems which require grading procedures for certification, for completion, for degree granting, and so on. In these cases, the evaluation techniques should be more formal (self-evaluation can still be used) and structured. This chapter will describe a variety of techniques that can be used both formally and informally in sessions with adult learners.

Evaluation is a component of the teaching and learning process which inevitably raises issues and concerns. As Brookfield states, "Attesting to the need for evaluation is somewhat akin to deciding to take exercise more regularly. Both are resolutions that are deemed important and necessary, but both are, for whatever reasons, rarely implemented" (Brookfield 1986, 261). Some of the common concerns will be addressed here.

Evaluation of learning is *not* synonymous with testing or grading. Evaluation implies a judgement of quality or degree; it may or may not include testing (i.e. a structured instrument) or grading (the assignment of a number or letter to that judgement). Evaluation, in some sense, always occurs in an instructional situation; however, testing or grading may not occur. It is important to realize the distinctions among these terms and not fall into the trap of saying, "I can't test this learning," or "I won't be grading this objective, therefore I am not evaluating it." If an objective is not being evaluated, or if in other words, you or your participants don't care whether or not that learning occurs, then it is not an objective.

Evaluation (or testing or grading) is sometimes opposed on the grounds that it merely produces anxiety and frustration among adult learners, and hence acts as a deterrent to the learning process. Again, this reaction is based on a misconception about the nature of evaluation. Indeed, if learners receive little or no feedback throughout instruction, then anxiety may occur. Frequent and regular feedback improves performance and facilitates learning. A formal written test will frighten the adult who has been away from instructional settings for several years and should not be used with any audience that has this characteristic. But this does *not* mean that evaluation of learning cannot occur. Alternatives to tests will be discussed in the section, *Evaluation and the Adult Learner*.

It may seem that some types of learning cannot be evaluated or can only be evaluated long after the instruction is over. How do we know, for example, that our nursing students will actually implement safe practice in the field, or that participants in a literature series will continue to read good books? How can we be sure that a learner actually enjoys or appreciates classical music instead of merely expressing enjoyment or appreciation because it is expected? Admittedly, there are many areas of learning that are difficult to evaluate. There are several aspects involved in this issue. One is matching an appropriate evaluation technique to the type of learning; for example, complex skills or values cannot be assessed with a multiple choice test. Second, in the statement of objectives, it is important at the earliest stages of planning to consider what behaviors indicate or represent the expected learning. Third, the long-term effects of instruction (or the predictive validity of evaluation techniques) is a subject for educational researchers and is most often beyond the direct responsibilities of the instructor. And finally, any measurement or evaluation technique contains some degree of error. Many factors influence a learner's response or an instructor's assessment of performance; it is not possible to assign a number or a grade that completely reflects true performance. This error of measurement must always be taken into account when decisions are being made, based on evaluation results.

The most important point to be made concerning evaluation of learning has to do with the information that is provided to both learners and instructor. It is difficult to imagine trying to learn to perform a task without knowing, in any way, whether or not you are successfully, or nearly successfully, completing some parts of it. If you are blindfolded, trying to find a particular object, and no one is telling you how close you are to it, you will only find it by chance, if at all. Learning relies on feedback, and it is evaluation that provides the feedback.

In summary, evaluation of learning is, by definition, a component of the instructional process. It does not necessarily involve the traditional test or examination situation, but in order to make any statement as to the effect of the instruction, some judgement of learning must be made. Evaluation procedures are complex, and it must be recognized that there cannot be a true assessment of someone's knowledge, skill, or value development. In spite of these difficulties, it is essential for both the instructor and the learner to be aware of the progress that is being made. Learners, on the basis of feedback, can review or practice or move on to other areas; instructors can provide supplemental resources or revise the instruction or feel pleased about a job well-done.

Evaluation Approaches

Before specific techniques are constructed, it is valuable to consider the general approach that will be taken toward the evaluation of learning. To some extent, the approach will affect both the type and the format of the evaluation procedures used in an instructional situation. The two basic approaches to evaluation of learning have been labelled norm-referenced and criterion-referenced evaluation. They often overlap in practice, but a description of each will be presented first, followed by practical examples.

Norm-Referenced Evaluation

Norm-referenced evaluation is the approach that is traditionally associated with testing and measurement. The scores that individuals receive are meaningful in comparison to other individuals or in comparison to a norm group (hence the label attached to this approach). All standardized tests for which norms have been established (achievement tests, aptitude inventories, intelligence tests, personality inventories) are examples of norm-referenced evaluation. Individuals are compared, in these examples, to a norm based on the evaluation of thousands of individuals who are comparable in age, education level, and cultural and language background. Adult educators who work in the health professions or in the trades, among other areas, will be familiar with the certification examinations that their students face at the end of a program; these are norm-referenced tests. When evaluation techniques are designed by the instructor, comparisons are usually made with the mean or average of that group. Most of us have probably experienced the "grading on a curve" phenomenon in college or university-level courses; this is an application of the norm-referenced approach. The approach yields statements such as, "the learner is above the mean for this test"; the individual is in the top 10% of the group"; or "this person has performed better than that person."

This approach "feels" wrong to almost every adult educator, unless he or she happens to be involved in certification procedures. Indeed, it is not usually appropriate in an individual class, session, course, or workshop. However, institutional constraints often force instructors into a grading procedure which resembles norm-referenced evaluation (the administrator who says, "you can't give all A's"). Also, the assessment of individuals on standardized instruments *can* be useful, for example, in determining aptitude, literacy levels, personality types. And finally, learners who will have to deal with certification examinations should be provided with the opportunity to practice the skills involved in such evaluation procedures and should receive feedback as to where they stand relative to other learners.

The purpose of norm-referenced evaluation is to discriminate among individuals on the basis of what they have learned. It is appropriate in situations where a predetermined number of people must be selected for remedial or advanced programs, for certification, or for placement. The norm-referenced test tends to be relatively long (to increase the accuracy of the discrimination) and is not necessarily associated directly with a set of objectives.

Criterion-Referenced Evaluation

The concept of criterion-referenced evaluation is relatively recent in the educational literature; it is commonly associated with individualized instruction or "mastery learning." As this implies, criterion-referenced evaluation is not concerned with comparisons among individuals, but rather with the learner's mastery of an objective or set of objectives. Hence, a test score is compared only to a cut-off score which has been selected as indicative of mastery of the content. Published criterion-referenced tests are usually a part of an individualized learning package. Criterion or cut-off scores are predetermined in a variety of ways, dependent on the subject area and the purpose of the package. Each test is relatively short, often about 10 items, and is designed to assess mastery of a specific objective. Criterion-referenced evaluation procedures developed by an instructor have the same format and purpose. No comparisons are made among learners. Results yield only the statement, "This individual has (or has not) mastered this objective or set of objectives."

The criterion-referenced approach most closely matches adult education strategies and is most likely to be appropriate to the characteristics of the adult learner. In any instructional situation, we wish to know whether the individual has learned, but we are less interested in how one individual's performance compares to another.

Evaluation and the Adult Learner

In the adult education literature, evaluation of learning is most often described as a fairly informal process. Most authors recommend that the adult learner evaluate his or her own learning, or that contracts be used in which the instructor and learner negotiate and agree upon work to be accomplished. Knowles provides the following comment:

> This is the easiest section of this whole book to write, for all I really have to say is to go back to the earlier section of this chapter on "Providing Evidence of Present Performance" and review the procedures suggested there for diagnosing the gaps between desired behavior and present performance. Evaluation of learning consists of repeating these procedures (or equivalent forms of them) and measuring the changes that have occurred (Knowles 1980, 247).

In his discussion of assessing present performance, the techniques are "self-diagnostic."

In many adult education settings, Knowles' model *is* appropriate. Workshops, interest sessions, tutoring, informal presentations, learning networks, community activities, and individual self-directed projects probably will emphasize self-evaluation through contracts or less structured techniques. However, even in these settings, when the audience do not have self-evaluation skills, the model may not be immediately feasible: adults in new situations will be anxious and dependent and will want someone else (the instructor) to tell them how they are doing. Self-evaluation and self-direction skills must be learned. The instructor can probably work toward this if he or she will be with the same audience over time.

On the other hand, a great deal of adult education takes place within the confines of a formal institution, which nearly always will have requirements regarding evaluation of learning. Brookfield (1986) lists the following formal settings: adult literacy and basic education; continuing professional education; labor education; universities, polytechnics and community colleges; and training in business and industry. In any setting where degrees, diplomas, or certificates are issued, or where certification examinations are required, or where administrative decisions such as salary increases and position promotions are linked to the evaluation results, the evaluation techniques are affected. This does not mean that formal examinations need to be used regularly in the instruction, but completely informal feedback techniques are not appropriate either.

The adult educator working within an institution or system requiring formal evaluation results or procedures faces a dilemma. The books on adult learning tell us that our participants should evaluate themselves, that no one should fail, that testing creates anxiety for the adult, and so on. And yet, we are required to turn in the marks at the end of the session.

Although there is great variation among settings (e.g. the instructor in the health professions being more constrained than the instructor in a graduate program), some general compromises that can be made in the face of this dilemma will be listed.

1. Allow participants input into the evaluation process in some way. This may simply involve providing a choice of activities, or it may include participants' suggesting, negotiating, or designing the projects or assignments upon which they will be evaluated.

2. Whenever possible, include some element of self-evaluation. For example, participants could evaluate their contribution to the group; they could evaluate one or two of their own papers or projects and negotiate any discrepancies with the instructor.

3. Suggest that participants work together in pairs or small groups on projects, assignments, papers, or other evaluation activities. They can either agree to accept the same grade, or negotiate an alternative among themselves, based on their contribution to the task. Of course, those who prefer independent activities should not be forced into group work.

4. Even if an in-class evaluation activity is conducted, suggest that participants work together in pairs or small groups.

5. If learners will be facing certification examinations, provide as much practice as possible with the testing format that will be used in the examination.

6. Encourage participants to select their own "weights" for the evaluation activities within a course. The instructor can provide an acceptable range of weights, if desired.

If some or all of these guidelines are implemented, the anxiety that the adult learner feels about evaluation will be eased to some extent. Above all, it is essential to be consistent, fair, and supportive with the adult who is threatened by evaluation.

The remainder of this chapter will deal with techniques for evaluating learning. Any technique can be used in a formal or an informal way; a multiple choice test can be used as a self-diagnostic instrument or as a formal test, and the same holds true for any of the testing formats.

Types of Testing Techniques

Regardless of the approach taken in the evaluation of learning, the technique may have several formats. Most of these (multiple choice, essays) are familiar to every educator and every learner in North America. It is important, however, to review the alternatives that are available and to consider which formats are appropriate in a particular instructional situation. This section will briefly describe the types of testing techniques, and the following section will discuss the selection of appropriate techniques.

Testing procedures can be divided into two categories: objectively scored tests and subjectively scored tests.

Objectively Scored Tests

As the label implies, objectively scored tests are ones in which each question or item has only one right answer; any two individuals who are scoring answers using a prepared answer key will obtain the same results. This type of test is sometimes called an objective test, a name which can be misleading: the items themselves may not be objective (that depends on the skill of the test developer). Four commonly used objectively scored test formats are: multiple choice, true/false, matching, and short answer.

Multiple choice tests. The multiple choice item consists of a statement or question, called the "stem," followed by a set of alternative endings to the statement or answers to the question. The wrong alternatives are called "distractors" and most often range in number from two to four. The items should have clear unambiguous stems with correct answers that are not a matter of opinion or controversy. The distractors should be short, plausible, and grammatically consistent with each other and the stem. The correct answer should be clearly right, not merely close or best. Specific guidelines for developing items will be presented later in this chapter.

Multiple choice tests can efficiently assess mastery of a large number of objectives. They are quick to score and measure the learner's knowledge without being influenced by writing or verbal ability. On the other hand, good multiple choice items are very difficult and time-consuming to construct. There is an opportunity for individuals to guess the correct response; there is no room for elaboration on the responses. The multiple choice test rarely, if ever, adequately assesses learning at the higher levels of the cognitive domain (analysis, synthesis, evaluation) or learning in the affective or psychomotor domains. Some authors (e.g. Green, 1975) argue that a cleverly constructed multiple choice item can assess any level of cognitive learning; however, the requirement of the task is the selection of an alternative, and the instructor cannot observe the process by which that selection is made.

Example 1:
Why do living organisms need oxygen?
a. to purify the blood
b. to oxidize waste
c. to release energy
d. to assimilate food
e. to fight infection

This item illustrates the question-style stem, stated clearly and concisely. The alternatives are grammatically parallel, short, and are all plausible to the learner who is unaware of the correct response.

Example 2:
The objective, "The student will be able to write a critique of John Fowles' *Mantissa*, based on the criteria of effective style, plot development and characterization" is an example of:
a. knowledge level learning
b. analysis level learning
c. synthesis level learning
d. evaluation level learning

This example contains an incomplete statement as a stem and illustrates the item characteristics described above.

True/false tests. A true/false test consists of a series of statements which the learner labels as true or false. Statements must be concise, straightforward, and clearly statements of fact, without qualifiers or stated opinions or attitudes (unless attributed to a writer (e.g. "Skinner (1972) stated that..."). Since guessing the answer by the learner is obviously a disadvantage of using this format, some variations have been developed in which the respondent is asked to explain why the item is false, or to underline those words or phrases that make the statement false. Some writers advocate the use of "right minus wrong" scoring techniques in order to discourage guessing; however the anxiety created by this procedure probably causes as much interference with accurate assessment as does unpenalized guessing.

True/false tests efficiently assess mastery of a large number of objectives and are quick to score. Individuals who lack verbal or writing ability are not assessed unfairly. However, the guessing factor decreases the accuracy of the assessment, and the true/false test is only appropriate for the knowledge or comprehension levels of the cognitive domain.

Example 1:

If the discriminant is negative, a quadratic equation has   T F
no real roots.

This item illustrates a straightforward, factual statement in which there is no ambiguity or opinion. It measures mastery of an objective at the comprehension level of the cognitive domain.

Example 2:

In September 1982, the Israeli government accepted the   T F
blame for the slaughter in West Beirut. (If false, underline
the word(s) that make the statement false).

In this example, the effect of guessing is counteracted by asking the learner to underline the part of the statement that makes it false, if that option is chosen. Since there are several possible phrases that could be false (the date, the countries, the verb"accept"), the instructor will have more confidence in the accuracy of the assessment.

Matching tests. A matching test consists of two columns of names, dates, definitions, etc., which must be correctly matched—one item from one column with the corresponding item from the second column. The columns are usually of different lengths to discourage guessing by elimination.

The advantages and disadvantages of the matching test are similar to those mentioned for multiple choice and true/false formats. However, the matching test does not tend to be as useful in the assessment of a wide array of objectives, and it is generally only appropriate at the knowledge level of the cognitive domain.

Example 1:

For each of the European novelists listed below on the left side, choose the title of the corresponding novel and put the appropriate letter beside the author's name.

___ 1. Turgenev	a. Buddenbrooks
___ 2. Hesse	b. Germinal
___ 3. Malraux	c. Fathers and Sons
___ 4. Mann	d. Nausea
___ 5. Silone	e. Bread and Wine
___ 6. Tolstoy	f. Steppenwolf
___ 7. Zola	g. Brothers Karamazov
___ 8. Camus	h. Man's Fate
	i. The Outsider
	j. War and Peace
	k. Madame Bovary

This example illustrates a straightforward matching of titles and authors. It is obvious that the item is assessing learning at the knowledge level of the cognitive domain. More titles than authors are listed, and the incorrect titles are plausible to the uninformed respondent.

Example 2:

For each of the terms listed on the left, select the appropriate definition and place the letter next to the term.

___ 1. external validity
___ 2. experimental group
___ 3. independent variable
___ 4. criterion variable
___ 5. reliability
___ 6. structural variable
___ 7. subject variable
___ 8. stratum
___ 9. dependent variable
___10. control group

a. subjects to whom no experimental treatment is administered
b. a valid, accepted measure of some trait
c. the variable that indicates response to treatment
d. the degree to which items correlate with each other
e. research participants exposed to the stimulus under study
f. generalizability of research findings
g. the variable that is manipulated
h. the abstract concepts used in theories
i. the consistency in results of a test
j. some subdivision of a population
k. in data analysis, a characteristic formed by combining units
l. a variable that is a property of a person

This example is a slightly more complex use of the matching item and dependent on the content of the instruction, could provide an assessment of the comprehension level of the cognitive domain. In this item, it should be noted that the comprehension of several different concepts (types of variables, reliability, validity) is being measured. It is important therefore that the list of definitions contain some plausible distractors and also that they use a wording that does not allow the learner to make the correct match without understanding the concept. Writing a matching item of this type requires a skill similar to that used in constructing multiple choice items (detailed guidelines will be provided in a later section of this chapter).

Short answer tests. The objectively scored short answer item consists of either a question for which only one word or phrase of a prespecified list of words or phrases is the correct response, or a statement in which the respondent is requested to fill in missing words or phrases. In either case, in order to meet the criteria of being objectively scoreable, the short answer must be unambiguously correct or incorrect.

In addition to the advantages listed for the previous objectively scored tests, the short answer test has the added benefit of requiring the learner to generate the correct response, as opposed to recognizing it. If items are rephrased from the wording used in the instruction or in readings, the short answer test usually assesses learning at the comprehension level of the cognitive domain. Also, in some subject areas (e.g. mathematics, computer science, statistics), the short answer test is often used at the application level of the cognitive domain.

Example 1:
According to Krathwohl et al. (1964), the five levels of learning of the affective domain are:

_____

_____

_____

_____

This example is a statement-completion item, probably assessing learning at the knowledge level of the cognitive domain. Note that the authority upon which the information is based is cited and that the learner is informed of the number of responses.

Example 2:
Calculate (rounding to one decimal point) the mean and standard deviation of the following set of test scores:
42, 57, 66, 66, 68, 72, 75, 75, 91.
Mean: _____
Standard deviation: _____

Although still an objectively scored item, this example illustrates assessment of learning at the application level of the cognitive domain. When learners are asked to show their work, and partial marks based on instructor judgement are given for this work, the short answer test becomes subjectively scored.

Subjectively Scored Tests

Subjectively scored tests include all evaluation techniques which rely on the judgement of the instructor for scoring. As such, they include a much more diverse set of procedures than do objectively scored tests: verbal or written learner responses; products such as paintings, crafts, or architectural blueprints; and, performances such as interviewing skill, playing squash, or laboratory experimentation. It is often feasible and always desirable to make these evaluation procedures as objective as possible (techniques will be discussed in detail later in this chapter); however some element of judgement does remain. Subjectively scored tests are used to assess learning in the higher levels of the cognitive domain (application, analysis, synthesis, and evaluation), in the affective domain, and in the psychomotor domain. The types of test formats will be divided into: essay format, oral format, checklists, rating scales, and comments or anecdotal information. These techniques can be grouped in a variety of ways as can be seen in books or articles on evaluation of learning; the relationships with other categorization systems will be presented as necessary.

Essay tests. The essay format consists of one or more questions or topics to which the learner responds in writing. The essay can range from a short or restricted format (requesting a paragraph, an outline, or a few pages) to a longer or unrestricted format yielding a paper of 50 or more pages, a project, a thesis, etc. The essay may be completed in a classroom (with or without the use of resource materials), or it may be completed independently or in groups outside the classroom over a period of time and utilizing a variety of materials. This technique is particularly appropriate for assessing learning in the higher levels of the cognitive and affective domains.

The essay allows an in-depth examination of learners' understanding of a topic or subject area. It allows individuals to express opinions and unique ideas and to elaborate on aspects of a topic in which they are interested. Often, several objectives from a segment of instruction can be assessed through one analytical or integrative essay topic. On the other hand, any instructor who has spent evenings reading essays or papers or projects is well aware of at least some of the disadvantages of this technique. Regardless of the amount of advance planning for scoring and/or feedback, the evaluation process is very time-consuming and difficult. It is often not possible to completely separate irrelevant variables (writing style, instructor opinion on the topic, neatness of the paper, predetermined attitudes toward the learner, etc.) from the actual content of the written material. Individuals who are working in a language other than their mother tongue or who have any other difficulties expressing themselves in writing may be unfairly evaluated using this technique. And finally, it is not usually possible with the essay format to evaluate learning in a wide variety of areas in a limited period of time.

Example 1:
Assuming that your reader has a background in psychoanalytic theory, describe in five to ten pages how Jung's ideas deviated from those of his mentor, Sigmund Freud. Where necessary, give references (a useful source will be the Freud-Jung letters in *Psychology Today*, distributed in class).

This item illustrates an unrestricted essay format, assessing learning at the analysis level of the cognitive domain. Learners are told clearly what is expected and material is referred to; however, the topic allows considerable variation in response.

Example 2:
Describe in one paragraph each, the lecture and the discussion methods of teaching (no more than 200 words per paragraph). Include in each description, examples of an instructional situation in which each method is appropriate.

This example is of the restricted essay type: there is little room for speculation or opinion. The type of learning measured would be the application level of the cognitive domain.

Example 3:
As a nursing student, you are caring for an elderly patient who is terminally ill with lung cancer. He is in pain and tells you that he refuses to take his medication, which you know is essential to his living. How would you respond to this patient?

This item is again unrestricted in format. It is assessing learning at the valuing level in the affective domain. Here the benefits of the essay response are clear: the learner is free to express feelings and unique strategies for dealing with the situation.

Oral tests. The oral test consists of a series of structured or semi-structured questions or a single question to which the learner responds verbally. Responses may be tape-recorded to facilitate evaluation and more than one instructor or examiner may be present. The most familiar oral tests include graduate studies comprehensive examinations or theses defences and assessments of second language learning. However, oral assessments may also take the form of interviews, discussions, or presentations. Whenever evaluation of learning is based on the verbal response of the learner, this evaluation can be called an oral test. Similar to the essay format, this technique is appropriate for evaluation in the higher levels of the cognitive and affective domains.

The advantages of the oral test are similar to those of the essay test: it allows an in-depth examination of learners' understanding, and it provides the opportunity for the expression of opinions and an elaboration on points of interest. In addition, when the learners' speaking ability is a component of the instruction, the oral test provides a valuable technique for assessment. The disadvantages of the oral test are again similar to those of the essay test but are exacerbated by the format. Scoring is subjective but is made more difficult (particularly when responses are not taped) by the nature of the evaluation situation. Checklists or rating scales (to be discussed later) can be used during the evaluation which partially overcomes this difficulty; however, instructors often feel that this detracts from the spontaneity of the interaction. Also, evaluations are often influenced by irrelevant learner characteristics such as appearance, interpersonal skill, and verbal ability. Each of these characteristics may also be skills that are being evaluated, in which case they are not irrelevant! Finally, the adult learner's anxiety is often high in an oral evaluation situation, and this can obviously interfere with an accurate assessment of learning.

Example 1:

After Cronbach's (1957) American Psychological Association presidential address, educational researchers began to look for aptitude-treatment interactions. However it was concluded after nearly 20 years that this line of investigation had "failed." Discuss, in 10 minutes, whether or not you agree with this conclusion and why, in your opinion, the research has failed or not failed. At the end of your discussion, the committee will have the opportunity to ask you further questions.

This example provides a clear topic for discussion and yet allows an unrestricted response; that is, the respondent is free to state opinions and to elaborate on points of interest. At the end of the presentation, an opportunity is provided for the evaluators to probe or ask further questions.

Example 2:

In the groups to which you have been assigned (four individuals per group), discuss the following issue: how would you, in your social work field experience, counsel an unmarried woman of 26 years of age who was deciding whether or not to have a tubal ligation performed? Discuss the characteristics of the client's lifestyle which might influence your counselling. You have fifteen minutes.

This example illustrates the use of interaction among learners. Although evaluation of individual learning becomes more difficult, the learners often feel less anxious and are stimulated by the discussion with their peers.

Checklists. Up to this point, the evaluation techniques presented have been appropriate for the cognitive and affective domains of learning. Evaluation of learning in the psychomotor domain involves observation of performance or the product of the performance. Observation, in itself, does not yield evaluation information; the observations should be recorded in an appropriate way. Checklists are used when the instructor intends to record the occurrence, or the frequency of occurrences of behaviors in a performance, or the existence of characteristics of a product. A checklist is simply a list of observable behaviors or characteristics which are checked off as they occur. There is no opportunity for ratings or judgements of quality, only whether or not the item was observed.

The checklist provides a structured and relatively objective technique for conducting observations of psychomotor or affective learning. It is possible to record and evaluate several behaviors or characteristics in one session. The checklist tends to be easy to construct and use. It is important to use the checklist only when the degree of quality of performance is not relevant to the evaluation.

Example 1:

	Met	Not Met
1. All caries and defective areas removed	____	____
2. Cavity preparation is clean	____	____
3. Adjacent tooth is undamaged	____	____

This example is a segment of a checklist used in a preclinical (laboratory) dental course. The product of the learner's performance is evaluated by the instructor, using a ten-item checklist. Although different performances may exhibit varying quality, the skills involved are viewed as having only one acceptable standard; hence, the checklist is the most efficient technique for evaluation.

Example 2:

____ 1. Doctor's orders are checked.
____ 2. Name of drug is checked.
____ 3. Time that drug is to be given is checked.
____ 4. Amount of drug to be given is checked.
____ 5. Method of giving drug is checked.
____ 6. Patient's name is checked.

This example is an excerpt from a checklist used to evaluate learner performance in administering a medication in a college-level nursing course. The assessed behaviors are of the kind that either exist or do not exist; no degree of quality of performance is observed.

Rating scales. In the evaluation of psychomotor learning the instructor is often concerned with the quality of the performance. Thus, a rating scale is commonly used. A rating scale consists of a list of behaviors or characteristics expressed in observable terms. A scale is used to indicate the quality or frequency of the behavior or the characteristic; for example, Outstanding, Good, Satisfactory, Poor; Always, Often, Sometimes, Never.

The rating scale provides a structured method for recording observations of psychomotor or affective learning. Several aspects of the performance can be evaluated in one session. The added judgement of quality or frequency increases, however, the subjectivity of the technique. The judgement of performance at the Olympic gymnastic competitions illustrates the difficulty. Several judges, viewing the same performance, will inevitably assign different numbers to the individual. Techniques for assessing this aspect of the rating procedure (inter-rater reliability) will be discussed later in the chapter.

Example 1:
Indicate the extent to which you agree or disagree with each of the statements listed below. Consider only the performance which you are observing on this occasion.
Scale:
1. Strongly Disagree / 2. Disagree / 3. Agree / 4. Strongly Agree

The student teacher:
1. Responds clearly to questions   1 2 3 4
2. States expectations of students   1 2 3 4
3. Distinguishes between major and
   minor topics   1 2 3 4
4. Summarizes major topics   1 2 3 4

This example is a segment of a rating scale which could be used in the evaluation of student teachers' performance in the classroom. The evaluator is assessing how well the student teacher performs, using a four-point scale. The items themselves may sometimes contain judgemental words such as "clearly" (Item 1); however, they should be kept at a minimum as they introduce another element of subjectivity.

Example 2:

1. Outline of occlusal portion is rounded with no sharp
   curves   A B C D E
2. Dimension of occlusal outline and isthmus is 1/4
   intercuspal distance   A B C D E
3. Pulpal depth is 1.5 to 2.0 mm.   A B C D E
4. Each cavity wall of proximal portion clears adjacent tooth
   by 0.25 to 0.5 mm.   A B C D E

Scale:

A Unacceptable; a significant error is made and cannot be
   corrected
B Satisfactory; there is a significant error which is
   biologically or mechanically detrimental but can be
   corrected; minimally clinically acceptable
C Satisfactory; an error is detected which is not biologically
   or mechanically detrimental and is clinically acceptable or
   uncorrectable; or clinically unacceptable but readily
   correctable
D Satisfactory; an error is detected that slightly departs
   from the ideal
E Excellent; there is no discernable error

This example is a segment of a rating scale used in a preclinical (laboratory) dentistry course. The instrument illustrates the design of a response scale which is specific to the instructional content. Note that the usual order of letters used (A through E) is reversed in an attempt to avoid a rater "response set" (a reliance on preconceived meanings for the points on a scale).

Example 3:

For each of the following statements indicate the extent to which you agree or disagree, using the scale below. Please indicate honestly how *you feel*. There are no right or wrong answers.
Scale:
1. Strongly Disagree / 2. Disagree / 3. Agree / 4. Strongly Agree

1. I feel responsible for any mistakes I make.
2. If I don't like people, I would have trouble interacting
   with them professionally.
3. If someone asked me a specific question about a patient, I
   would most likely answer it.
4. If possible, I would involve a patient in a decision
   concerning him or her.
5. It is not my place, as a student, to make decisions.

This example is taken from an assessment of students' affective learning in a department of nursing at the college level. It illustrates a different use of the rating scale: learners are responding to the items rather than instructors or observers. The purpose of the instrument is to evaluate values and beliefs.

Comments, anecdotal records, journals. This last category of subjectively scored evaluation techniques is usually the least structured and least formal means of collecting information and providing feedback to learners. Either learners or instructor record in some prespecified format what learning is taking place, how they feel about an instructional situation, or any other relevant details.

One commonly used technique in this category is the journal. In a situation where the instructor is unable to participate in or observe the learning experiences, the learner can keep a journal or diary containing a description of the activities and the learning which occurred. A social work student who participates in volunteer field work could be asked to record the interactions with the client and to describe any applications of theories studied. A second useful technique is the keeping of anecdotal records by the instructor. In a group where participation or interaction among individuals is one of the components of the evaluation of learning, the instructor may wish to regularly record the degree to which individuals participate and possibly the content or quality of their contributions.

The use of comments, anecdotal records, and journals has several advantages. Where the instructor cannot observe learner activities, these evaluation techniques can be used to provide information about the type and amount of learning (this tends to be particularly valuable in the affective domain). Also, where it may be difficult or too subjective a process to retrospectively consider learner involvement or activity, instructor-kept records can facilitate evaluation. Generally, this allows the collection of detailed and in-depth information. The major disadvantage clearly lies in the use and interpretation of the information. Even more so than the essay or oral test, the analysis of comments or journals is a difficult task. Second, particularly in the evaluation of affective learning, individuals may respond to perceived instructor expectations, and instructors may be affected by irrelevant variables, such as learners' verbal ability or instructors' own values or attitudes.

Example 1:

In your journal, record at the end of each volunteer experience, your interaction with the client and how you felt or what you learned. Use the format illustrated below. Each Friday give your week's journal to your instructor for comments and feedback.

Record of Interaction	How I felt/What I learned
Client:	
Me:	
Client:	
Me:	

This example, taken from a first-year Skills Lab in a School of Social Work, illustrates a semi-structured journal. Learners are not expected to recall word for word their dialogue with a client; however, it is felt that this remembering process is also a required professional skill. In the second column, learners are encouraged to record any cognitive (e.g. what skill they were using) or affective (e.g. their personal reaction to the situation) learning. Journals are not usually assigned grades, but detailed formative feedback is given by the instructor each week.

Example 2:

Date	Name	Comment on Contribution

This example illustrates an anecdotal record form which could be used by an instructor who was interested in the frequency and nature of individuals' contributions to group discussions. Such a record could form a component of the evaluation for grading purposes, if this was relevant, or could be used to give feedback to individuals on their contributions.

Summary

Each of the evaluation techniques discussed in this section has advantages and disadvantages. Generally, when the technique provides more in-depth information or is more useful for higher level or complex learning, the scoring and interpretation is more difficult. When the instrument can be objectively scored, it tends to be limited to use with the lower levels of learning and also to be more time-consuming to construct.

In the next section of this chapter, the matching of test types to the instructional situation will be discussed.

Selecting the Appropriate Evaluation Technique

A wide variety of evaluation techniques has been described. In some cases, the selection of a technique for the assessment of learning may seem straightforward; however, several variables influence this decision. The appropriateness of a particular format may be dependent to varying degrees on: the domain and level of expected learning; practical considerations such as group size, facilities, time limitations, or certification requirements; and special audience characteristics such as verbal ability, special needs, age, or previous test experience. This section will present guidelines for the selection of the type of evaluation format. It is important, too, to remember that there are no absolute formulae and that more than one technique may be appropriate for a particular instructional situation.

Domain and Level of Learning

If extreme examples are considered, common sense reveals that certain evaluation formats cannot be used for some types of learning: no one would consider evaluating diving performance with a multiple choice test or an individual's knowledge of terms with a rating scale. In many instructional situations, however, the decision is not that clear.

Table 6-1 presents a matrix of the cognitive levels of learning by testing techniques. Each type of test is described as "always appropriate" for the level of learning (Yes); "can be appropriate in some situations" (Maybe); or "never appropriate" (No). Note that there are several formats that are described as "always appropriate" for some of the levels of learning; for example, all of the objectively scored tests are appropriate for the knowledge and comprehension levels of the cognitive domain. In these cases, the decision as to which format will be used would depend on instructor preference or audience characteristics.

Where a testing technique is described as "can be appropriate in some situations," the decision usually depends on the subject area, the level of instruction, audience characteristics, or perhaps on the instructor's skill at item-writing. For example, a skilled item-writer, working in a structured subject area could make use of multiple choice items for the analysis level of the cognitive domain; however, in most cases, this would not be appropriate. The use of checklists or rating scales to evaluate learning in the cognitive domain would also be rarely used—perhaps only where cognitive learning is revealed through performance, such as in health professions training.

Table 6-2 presents the same matrix for the levels of learning in the affective domain. Here the objectively scored techniques are only useful at the lower levels, and it is unlikely that either true/false items or

TABLE 6–1: Appropriateness of Testing Techniques in Cognitive Domain

LEVELS OF DOMAIN	TYPES OF TESTS								
	Multiple Choice	True/ False	Matching	Short Answer	Essay Test	Oral Test	Checklist	Rating Scale	Comments Anecdotal
Knowledge	Yes	Yes	Yes	Yes	No	No	Maybe	No	Maybe
Comprehension	Yes	Yes	Yes	Yes	No	No	Maybe	No	Maybe
Application	Yes	No	No	Yes	Maybe	Maybe	Maybe	Maybe	Yes
Analysis	Maybe	No	No	Maybe	Yes	Yes	No	Maybe	Yes
Synthesis	No	No	No	No	Yes	Yes	No	Maybe	Yes
Evaluation	No	No	No	No	Yes	Yes	No	Maybe	Yes

Yes = Always Appropriate
Maybe = Can be Appropriate in Some Situations
No = Never Appropriate

TABLE 6–2: Appropriateness of Testing Techniques in The Affective Domain

					TYPES OF TESTS					
LEVELS OF DOMAIN	Multiple Choice	True/ False	Matching	Short Answer	Essay Test	Oral Test	Checklist	Rating Scale	Comments Anecdotal	
Receiving	Yes	Maybe	Maybe	Yes	No	No	Yes	No	Yes	
Responding	Yes	No	No	Maybe	Maybe	Maybe	Yes	No	Yes	
Valuing	Maybe	No	No	No	Yes	Yes	Yes	Yes	Yes	
Organization	No	No	No	No	Yes	Yes	No	Yes	Yes	
Value complex	No	No	No	No	Yes	Yes	No	Yes	Yes	

Yes = Always Appropriate
Maybe = Can be Appropriate in Some Situations
No = Never Appropriate

TABLE 6–3: Appropriateness of Testing Techniques in the Psychomotor Domain

LEVELS OF DOMAIN	TYPES OF TESTS									
	Multiple Choice	True/ False	Matching	Short Answer	Essay Test	Oral Test	Checklist	Rating Scale	Comments Anecdotal
Perception	No	No	No	No	No	No	Maybe	Maybe	Maybe
Set	No	No	No	No	No	No	Maybe	Maybe	Maybe
Guided Reponse	No	No	No	No	No	Maybe	Maybe	Maybe	Yes
Mechanism	No	No	No	No	No	Maybe	Maybe	Maybe	Yes
Complex Overt Response	No	No	No	No	No	Maybe	Maybe	Yes	Yes
Adaptation	No	No	No	No	No	Maybe	No	Yes	Yes
Origination	No	No	No	No	No	Maybe	No	Yes	Yes

Yes = Always Appropriate
Maybe = Can be Appropriate in Some Situations
No = Never Appropriate

matching items would be used at all. The essay and oral test formats are appropriate at the higher levels of learning. Observation techniques (checklists, rating scales, anecdotal records) are generally useful.

Table 6-3 contains the matrix of psychomotor levels of learning by testing techniques. Here, none of the paper and pencil techniques are described as being appropriate. Although these techniques may be used in a learning situation that is predominately psychomotor in nature, they should only be used to assess the overlap with the cognitive domain or the affective domain (e.g. describing the scoring system for a squash game or outlining the steps in conducting a physical examination in medicine). The series of "Maybe's" given for the oral test refer to its use in instructional situations where speech or oral ability are a part of the desired learning (second language learning, drama). In most cases, observation of either the performance or the product of the performance is the only appropriate evaluation technique. Depending on whether or not degrees of quality of performance exist in the particular skill, the instructor would turn to either checklists or rating scales. At the highest levels (adaptation and origination), some degree of quality is a part of the description of the learning. The checklist becomes inappropriate.

Practical Considerations

Very often the ideal choice of evaluation format must be modified due to practical considerations. If, for example, the instructor is working with objectives at the higher levels of the cognitive domain, but is presenting to a group of 100 individuals, the natural choice of oral or essay formats has obvious limitations. The most common practical considerations include: group size, facilities and resources, time restraints, and the requirements of professional associations or certification boards. Each of these will be discussed briefly in terms of the effect that they have on the choice of format, and some guidelines will be provided for modifying choices.

When the group size is large (over 50), the instructor is usually unable to use any subjectively scored format. This is a particularly difficult dilemma to deal with, and most often the instructor must compromise on some aspect of the decision—either using less than desirable techniques or devoting extensive time to providing feedback, marking, or managing the evaluation activity. Possible suggestions (their relevance is dependent on the subject area, facilities, and resources) are:

1. Use structured, restricted essay items in conjunction with a well-planned scoring system;

2. Have teaching aides or assistants provide feedback or score responses (with the use of detailed criteria and with some training or practice);

3. Have individuals in the group provide feedback and/or test scores for each other, using a standard system and randomly checking on the results; or

4. Combine short answer or multiple choice items with a small number of restricted essay items, attempting to assess all of the prerequisite lower-level objectives from your task analysis with the objectively scored items.

Facilities and resources become a consideration primarily in instructional situations where psychomotor learning is a major component of the curriculum. It is often the case, for example, that an instructor of nursing is responsible for teaching and evaluating several individuals, each of whom could be performing different tasks. In other subject areas, the instructor may not have adequate facilities to actually allow each individual to perform a task (e.g. a shortage of laboratory equipment). The following options might be useful to the instructor who must compensate for such limitations:

1. Use simulations or role-playing to evaluate performance (but keep in mind that performance in the real setting may be slightly different);

2. Have learners share equipment in pairs: one person can be the performer for one task while the other evaluates the performance, reverse the roles for the next task;

3. Have individuals work in small groups to complete a project using the same material, equipment, or resources, and provide evaluation of the group's performance; or

4. Use journals in situations where you are unable to observe individual performance; have the learner record each step of the performance, possibly including his or her own reactions or a self-evaluation.

Time restraints (aside from the time required to score essay responses) can sometimes be an important consideration. For example, in the evaluation of psychomotor learning, using observation (rating scales or checklists) techniques, each individual is evaluated separately. For a complex or long performance, such an evaluation would require considerable instructor time. In other situations, the required evaluation could take excessive learner time (e.g. in the implementation of a programming technique which requires numerous lower-level steps). As in the other situations described so far, some compromise must usually be made in terms of the preferred evaluation technique. Suggestions include:

1. Rather than evaluating each individual's entire performance, sample the performance of each learner while several learners are engaged in the same task;

2. Whenever it is the case that the product of the performance will accurately reflect what the learner did, evaluate that aspect rather than the entire process; or

3. In cases where a large number of detailed lower-level steps are required of the learner (and these steps are not necessarily being evaluated), make that part of the process available to the learner and only evaluate the final steps.

The final practical consideration which is sometimes encountered is meeting the requirements of professional associations or certification boards. For example, in a trades program, the instructor may be teaching higher-level cognitive skills or psychomotor skills and therefore wish to utilize subjectively scored techniques; however, it is often the case that the certification examination is in multiple choice format. Instructors will then naturally feel obligated to use that format in order to prepare their students for these tests by using the same evaluation technique. At other times, instructors may be required by an external association or by administrators to give tests in a format which does not match the instructional situation. Relatively few options may be available:

1. To prepare learners for a particular test format, administer that format, but do not use the scores in any grading system;

2. Combine the required test format with your preferred format, using the former as appropriately as possible and giving it less weight in the grading procedure if necessary; or

3. Propose to external agencies or administrators that the required format be modified to suit the type of expected learning.

In general, practical considerations lead to some compromise of the principles discussed in the previous section. It is usually possible, however, to maintain some match between the evaluation technique and the type of expected learning.

Learner Characteristics

As has been discussed in previous chapters, the teaching and learning process is a complex interaction of many variables. In all aspects of instructional planning, characteristics of the audience must be considered. In choosing evaluation techniques for the adult learner, special care must be taken. The adult is likely to feel anxious or threatened in the face of being evaluated; encouraging success and providing support will be important. Even the word "test" should be avoided with the new adult learner. The instructor should always check how familiar the learner is with a specific format; if the adult has been away from instructional settings for some time, he or she may not have encountered certain evaluation formats. If language or literacy level seems likely to affect learner responses, this should also be taken into account.

Some guidelines are:

1. Assess the audience characteristics (either formally or informally) which you believe are relevant to the preferred evaluation technique;

2. If learners are exhibiting any language difficulties and if you find an essay format most appropriate, make every attempt to ignore grammar, spelling, or vocabulary deficiencies. Unless, of course, that is what you are teaching!

3. Consider using an oral format for those learners who exhibit severe writing deficiencies; this will allow you to ask probing questions in situations where language may be an obstacle, and to provide reassurance where the learner is anxious; or

4. When learners lack experience with a particular format, arrange practice sessions, and provide supportive feedback on learner responses.

When learners exhibit a learning or personality characteristic which is not relevant to the objectives or the instruction, every attempt must be made to not let that characteristic affect the evaluation.

Constructing Tests

So far, each of the evaluation formats has been described, and attention has been paid to the instructional situations in which each is appropriate. Regardless of the format, some general principles should always be adhered to.

1. An evaluation should assess what it is intended to assess. Although this may seem to be an obvious statement, instructors often make the mistake of, for example, assuming that because learners are able to recall a definition or a formula, they can also apply it in a problem-solving situation. The evaluation should always require that the learner exhibit the behavior which is described in the instructional objectives.

2. An evaluation should consistently assess learning. That is, items which are intended to measure the same objective should yield similar results. (There will be some variation due to errors or

other aspects of the situation.) In addition, the same evaluation performed at different times with the same learner should also produce similar results if no instruction has taken place.

3. Learners should always be aware of exactly what is expected in any evaluation situation. In order to ensure this, items must be clearly worded, and all expectations (length of response, degree of detail) and conditions (use of correct spelling, use of resources such as calculators or references) must be explicit and agreed upon.

4. Any scoring procedure, including any weighting system employed, should be agreed upon in advance and clearly described.

All evaluations should provide an accurate and reliable assessment of the expected learning, whether it is for feedback or for grading purposes. Specific guidelines for the construction of each of the test formats described earlier will be presented in the following sections.

Multiple Choice Tests

Writing good multiple choice items is one of the most difficult evaluation tasks. Any instructor who has used this technique will recall the frustrating difficulty of generating plausible distractors and wording the stem so that only one correct answer is possible. Generally, the development of items is a skill which requires practice and feedback from both learners and colleagues. The beginning item-writer should always have the test reviewed by a colleague and whenever possible, should give the items to one or two students who are familiar with the subject area for comment on clarity, difficulty level, etc.

Guidelines for the construction of multiple choice items are:

1. Present one clearly stated problem, statement, or question in the stem of the item;

2. Use simple, clear language with no subjective (e.g. "best") or controversial concepts;

3. Put as much as possible of the wording into the stem of the item, thereby avoiding redundant or complex distractors;

4. State the stem, wherever possible, in positive form (if negative wording must be used, emphasize it by underlining or capitalizing the negative words);

5. Ensure that all alternatives are grammatically consistent with the stem;

6. Avoid any verbal clues which might enable learners to select the correct answer or eliminate incorrect alternatives;

7. Develop distractors which are plausible and attractive to the learner who has not achieved the objective;

8. Vary the relative length of the correct alternative (there is tendency to add extra qualifications to the right answer);

9. Vary the position of the correct answer;

10. Avoid the use of "all of the above" as an alternative—it is generally not the correct answer, and if it is, the item format should be a short answer;

11. Avoid the use of "none of the above" as an alternative—it is rarely the correct answer and when it is, there is no certainty that learners *do* know the right answer; and

12. Design each item so that it is independent of other items on the test and contains no clues to answers of other items.

True/False Tests

True/false tests tend to be easier to construct than the multiple choice format, but as mentioned previously, their use tends to be limited to the knowledge and comprehension levels of the cognitive domain. Specific guidelines for the construction of items are:

1. Include in each statement only one concept which is clearly true or false;

2. Keep the statement short, using simple language and no complex grammatical structures;

3. Use negative statements sparingly and never use double negatives;

4. Avoid the use of qualifying words or phrases (e.g. "all," "never," "often") as they provide learners with a clue as to the correct response; and

5. Attribute statements of opinion to a specific source.

Matching Tests

The matching test can be constructed quickly and yields an efficient technique for the evaluation of knowledge of associations between sets of facts or concepts.

Guidelines for item construction are:

1. Use only homogeneous lists in each column of the item (e.g. historical events and the relevant dates, authors and titles, terms and definitions). If each list is not homogeneous, learners will be able to eliminate incorrect responses on that basis;

2. Use between five and fifteen items on each list; fewer items allow guessing and more items become confusing;

3. Arrange the response list (usually on the right hand side) in alphabetical or chronological order to facilitate the finding of the correct alternative;

4. Clearly indicate in the directions the basis upon which the matching is to be done; and

5. Have unequal numbers of items in the two lists in order to minimize guessing.

Short Answer Tests

Short answer tests are relatively easy to develop and also allow the instructor to evaluate learning which is at least at the application level of the cognitive domain. Items may have several formats: a direct question, an incomplete statement, a problem, a definition, or an identification. Regardless of the specific format, several guidelines should be applied to the item construction:

1. State the item so that only a single correct answer is possible;

2. Limit the length of the response to single words or short phrases; longer responses usually result in subjective scoring;

3. In incomplete statements, only omit significant or key words or phrases;

4. Do not provide grammatical clues as to the correct response;

5. When using the incomplete statement format, construct the statement so that the blank appears near the end;

6. Avoid using verbatim quotes from a textbook or reading; and

7. Prepare a scoring key in advance which includes all possible correct answers.

Essay Tests

Although it is relatively simple to construct, the essay test requires careful advance preparation for scoring; this process should be considered a part of the development of the technique. Two formats of essay tests are commonly used, those requiring restricted or extended responses. The following rules for construction apply to both formats:

1. Design each item to measure one or more well-defined learning outcomes;

2. Present a clear, definite task to the learner, one which is not open to different interpretations or approaches;

3. Include in the item any conditions or criteria which apply to the response (e.g. length, format, grammatical or spelling requirements);

4. Avoid the use of jargon and complex sentence structures;

5. In advance, write model answers for each item on the test; they may consist of complete responses or detailed outlines of the expected responses;

6. If possible, have a colleague review the model answers;

7. Devise a point system, based on the model answer, in which learners receive marks for each expected concept, argument, or other relevant attribute;

8. Evaluate all individuals' responses to one question before proceeding to the next question, as this tends to minimize the quality of one response affecting the scoring of the next question for an individual student; and

9. Provide detailed written feedback, describing strengths of work as well as suggestions for improvement.

Oral Tests

The construction and scoring of oral tests are similar to the procedures used with essay tests; however, there are additional difficulties arising from the observation of a live performance. It may be valuable to video-tape or tape-record responses to facilitate scoring and feedback.

Guidelines for the development and use of the oral test are:

1. Present the learner with a clear, well-defined task which is directly related to one or more objectives;

2. Design all questions so that they are comparable in length and difficulty, or evaluate all participants individually and independently using the same set of questions;

3. Circulate copies of the questions to be discussed to individuals in advance, unless skill in responding on the spot is being evaluated;

4. Clearly indicate the expected timing of the responses in advance;

5. When using a discussion or interview format, use objective, probing questions so as not to lead participants to the expected responses;

6. Attempt to reduce learner anxiety by speaking slowly and clearly and establishing a relaxed atmosphere;

7. Either tape-record, videotape, or take clear notes of learner responses;

8. Develop a clear set of criteria of performance based on the objectives that are being evaluated;

9. Consider converting the criteria into a checklist or rating scale (guidelines given in the next two sections) to be used either during the evaluation or when reviewing the recorded responses; and

10. When using this technique for summative evaluation, have more than one evaluator or instructor assess the responses.

Checklists

When the objectives for a task or performance are clearly stated, the construction of a checklist becomes relatively straightforward. Guidelines are:

1. Write short, clear, unambiguous items which are not open to more than one interpretation on the part of the observer;

2. Include only one behavior or characteristic in each item;

3. Design each item so that it is answerable in a "yes-no" format;

4. Keep the number of items to a minimum: checklists containing more than 15 items become unmanageable and hence unreliable; and

5. Organize items in a logical sequence to facilitate the observer's use of the checklist.

Rating Scales

Rating scales are used to enable the instructor to record systematically the quality of a performance or to evaluate learning in the affective domain by having individuals respond to the list of statements. The construction of a rating scale for either purpose is similar to the development of a checklist, the inclusion of a response scale being the major difference. Guidelines for the development of rating scales are:

1. Write clear, unambiguous items which are not open to observer or respondent interpretation;

2. Include only one behavior or characteristic in each item and base each item on an objective;

3. Design a response scale which matches the nature of the evaluation being done (either frequency, quality, or agreement);

4. Ensure that there are an equal number of positive and negative points on the scale (an unequal number will affect the accuracy of the rating);

5. Keep the number of items to a minimum: for use in observation, there should be less than 15 items and for a learner response scale, less than 30; and

6. Arrange items in a logical sequence and ensure that the format is not confusing.

Comments, Anecdotal Records, Journals

The use of comments, anecdotal records, and journals is an informal evaluation technique which requires careful planning in order to yield useful information. Although details will obviously vary according to the instructional situation, the purpose of the evaluation, and the objectives being assessed, general guidelines include:

1. Plan carefully in advance which behaviors, affective responses, etc., will be recorded, based on the objectives being evaluated;

2. Design a clear format for the recording of comments, providing complete directions for the use of the format;

3. Indicate clearly whether objective (i.e. only the "what" or "how" of the situation) or subjective (i.e. interpretations of the event) comments are to be recorded;

4. Describe the context in which the information is collected or ask learners to include this in their records if the instructor is not present;

5. Ensure that the recording occurs either during or as soon as possible after the event; and

6. If the records are intended to contribute to grades, plan in advance specific criteria that will be used in the analysis of the results (a system similar to that used in the scoring of essay tests is likely to be most useful).

Evaluating and Revising the Test

Once the techniques for evaluating learning have been developed, how can the instructor be assured that the technique is a good one? In practice, the instructor may not have the facilities or the time to formally assess the quality of the tests being used; however it is nearly always possible to collect some information which will lead to the improvement of the evaluation technique. A good test consistently and accurately assesses the learning that it is intended to assess. This definition contains two general concepts, reliability and validity, each of which will be defined. Specific procedures for evaluating the instructor-made test will be discussed.

Reliability

Reliability means, simply, consistency. Just as we expect a reliable car to start and to carry us to our destination, regardless of the weather or other circumstances, we expect a reliable test to yield stable and consistent results. It should not produce radically different results if it is administered to the same group of learners on two different occasions, or if it is scored by two different instructors. In the literature on test reliability, many different types of "consistency" are addressed, and sophisticated techniques for assessing reliability are presented. However, for the assessment of an instructor-made technique, one or more of three straightforward procedures are relevant.

Stability, or test-retest reliability refers to the degree to which an instrument will produce similar results on two different occasions when no relevant instruction has been provided in the intervening time. This does not sound like a practical thing to actually *do*, but the concept is important. If an instrument does not have test-retest reliability, it usually means that a variety of errors are occurring: learners are interpreting vague or ambiguous items; the test is influenced by irrelevant audience characteristics; or, the test is influenced by characteristics of the situation in which it is completed.

Internal consistency is the degree to which items intended to measure the same objective produce similar results. On many standardized published tests, it is expected that either all items on the test or all items on a sub-scale will be related to each other; in these cases, internal consistency is assessed by calculating correlations (relationships) among items. For practical reasons, the instructor-made test rarely contains more than two or three items assessing the same skill, and consequentially, internal consistency is more difficult to judge. When it is expected that learners who perform well on one item should also perform well on another item, this should be checked. Lack of consistency probably indicates that the items allow for more than one interpretation.

Inter-rater reliability is relevant whenever subjective judgements are made. It is assessed by the degree to which two or more raters or evaluators agree in their evaluation of a response (in an essay test, oral test, or in the observation of performance using a checklist or rating scale). Inter-rater reliability is usually assessed by calculating the correlation between scores produced by two individuals who are judging the same performance or product. Lack of agreement indicates that the evaluators are using criteria which are open to subjective interpretation.

Validity

A test is valid when it measures what it was intended to measure. Although this seems straightforward, the assessment of test validity is a complex process. A large literature is available, which discusses the various types of validity and techniques for their estimation. For the instructor-made test, one or more of four types of validity may be relevant, depending on the purpose of the evaluation and the type of test.

Content validity is the degree to which the test accurately represents the subject area or the instructional objectives. Regardless of the type of test, the common procedure for determining content validity is review by subject area experts. In the development of, for example, a college-level placement test for literacy skills, the test developers would consult several college English instructors, asking them to examine the instrument for comprehensiveness and relevance. An instructor who has constructed a new test could consult with individuals who teach in the same area. A copy of the instructional objectives and possibly a description of the teaching techniques should be provided to the reviewer and explicit instructions given as to the nature of the review. (E.g. Does this item assess learning of this objective?)

Concurrent validity is the extent to which two different measures of the same characteristic agree with each other when they are administered at the same or nearly the same time. To follow the previous example of the college-level literacy test, the test developers would expect that a sub-scale of the instrument, intended to assess grammatical skills, would be related to learners' use of grammar in a written composition. An instructor assessing concurrent validity would examine the relationship between evaluations measuring similar skills, or consider the agreement between test results and other observations of related performance. Any radical disagreement between different measures would be an indication that the test lacked concurrent validity, and further examination of the cause of this would be necessary.

Predictive validity is similar to concurrent validity (in fact, the two are often grouped together and called criterion validity). To assess predictive validity, one investigates the degree to which the test is related to (or predicts) future performance. It is expected, for example, that the Scholastic Aptitude Test predicts performance (grade point average) in graduate school. An instructor would expect that tests given throughout a semester would be related to performance on a final examination or a certification examination. Although predictive validity can only be assessed well after the test is administered, it is a useful judgement to make when the test will be reused over time.

Construct validity is a slightly more abstract concept. Generally, it means the degree to which test results are what would be expected based on underlying theoretical constructs. In the measurement of personality characteristics, for example, it may be expected on theoretical grounds that a relationship exists between anxiety and internal-external locus of control. If a new measure of test anxiety was developed, an assessment of construct validity could then include an investigation of the relationship between test results and results from an internal-external locus of control inventory. Dependent on the subject area, the instructor could utilize any known relationships among learning in different areas to check the construct validity of a new instrument.

Procedures for Test Review and Revision

Depending on the type of test, different procedures for test review and revision will be applicable. For the purposes of this discussion, test formats will be categorized into objectively scored formats, essay and oral tests, and observation techniques (rating scales and checklists).

Objectively scored tests. The first step in the assessment of any evaluation technique is the review process (content validity). For the objectively scored test, this process should include not only an assessment of the match of test items to objectives, but also an examination of the extent to which the items follow the guidelines for test construction given on pages 163 to 165. This review usually directly indicates the revisions to be made and occasionally results in discarding some items or changing an item format (e.g. multiple choice to short answer).

Once the test has been administered and results are available, further steps may be taken to assess the quality of the instrument. Item analysis is commonly done automatically if the test is computer scored; however the statistics are relatively easy to calculate by hand as well, and they provide valuable information. Item analysis yields information as to the difficulty of each item and the degree to which each discriminates among high and low achievers (or similarly, the degree to which each item is related to the total test score).

The *difficulty index* is simply the percentage of respondents who answered the item correctly. It may be reported as a percentage or in decimal format and is calculated by:

$$Difficulty = \frac{N(R)}{N}$$

where $N(R)$ is the number of individuals who responded correctly to the item, and where N is the total number of people taking the test.

When the test is norm-referenced, it is expected that the average difficulty index is about 0.5 or 50%; that is, when the test is used to make discriminations among learners, there should be both easy and difficult items in order to make distinctions at both the high and low levels of achievement. The difficulty of items should be fairly evenly distributed (easy, average, difficult), yielding the average of 0.5. However, when the test is criterion-referenced, as is often the case in adult education, quite different results would be expected. Remembering that the purpose of the criterion-referenced evaluation is to assess mastery of an objective rather than to discriminate among learners, the instructor would likely expect the average difficulty indices of items to be considerably higher than 0.5 to indicate that either the instruction was inadequate, or that the test was not accurately assessing the objectives. Although a general rule of thumb may not always apply, one could probably expect the difficulty indices to be about 0.8 or 80%. Ideally, the instructor should predict the difficulty of each item and base the revision of the item on discrepancies between expected and obtained indices.

Inappropriate or unexpected difficulty indices tend to be caused by one or more of the following:

1. use of complex or vague words or phrases in the item;

2. in the multiple choice format, either implausible distractors or more than one correct answer;

3. external cues which indicate the correct response; and

4. item wording taken directly from a textbook or reading.

Items should be carefully examined for these flaws, possibly with the assistance of colleagues. They may be either revised or discarded and replaced depending on the nature of the problem.

The *discrimination index*, although more difficult to calculate, is a straightforward concept and conveys important information. When an item discriminates among high and low achievers, it would be expected that the majority of the high achievers respond correctly and the majority of the low achievers respond incorrectly. To calculate this statistic, the following steps are taken:

1. Obtain the total test score for all learners;

2. Divide the group into thirds: the upper group, the middle group, and the lower group (based on the total test score); when the number of learners does not yield three equal groups, include the extras in the middle group; the upper and lower group must have equal numbers;

3. For each item, determine the number of learners in the upper group who responded correctly, and the number of learners in the lower group who responded correctly;

4. Calculate the discrimination index for each item using the following formula:

$$Discrimination\ Index = \frac{U - L}{N}$$

where U = Number of learners in the upper group who responded correctly, L = Number of learners in the lower group who responded correctly, and N = Number of students in *each* group.

It can be seen that if all learners in the upper group responded correctly and no learners in the lower group responded correctly, the index would be 1.0.

$$Discrimination\ Index = \frac{15 - 0}{15} = 1$$

Conversely, if no learners in the upper group responded correctly and all learners in the lower group responded correctly, the index would be -1.0.

$$Discrimination\ Index = \frac{0 - 15}{15} = -1$$

The index can range from +1 to –1, and the higher the number, the more the item discriminates between high and low achievers.

For a norm-referenced test, where discrimination among individuals is the purpose of the measurement, it is expected that the indices would be high. Generally, it is stated that a discrimination index for a norm-referenced evaluation should be at least +.3 and preferably higher. Any item below this level should be revised or discarded. For the criterion-referenced test, obviously, the interpretation of this statistic changes radically. Although it may be argued that the discrimination index should not be considered at all, useful information can be provided. If, for a criterion-referenced test, the discrimination index is negative, this could be a warning that the item is flawed (one still expects that the high achievers would tend to respond correctly). A discrimination index that is low, or near zero, is not a likely cause for alarm. It is usually the case that a small number of items (even one or two) measure mastery of one objective, and if objectives are relatively independent, any one individual could respond correctly to one item and not to another. Also, when the difficulty index is high (e.g. 80% or 90%), which is expected with the criterion-referenced approach, the small number of learners responding incorrectly will automatically lead to a low discrimination index. In fact, a high discrimination index might lead the instructor to question the effectiveness of the instruction for a portion of the audience. The instructor should predict in advance the expected indices and base the revision process on the discrepancy between predicted and obtained results.

An unexpected or unacceptable discrimination index could be caused by:

1. Implausible distractors (multiple choice format);

2. More than one correct or "best" answer (multiple choice format);

3. The existence of clues either within the item or in other items as to the correct response;

4. The use of wording directly from a textbook or reading;

5. The use of double negatives or any "trick wording" (these items measure a type of test-taking skill rather than learning); and

6. Lack of time to complete the test for some respondents.

The instructor should carefully review the problem items and in unclear cases, discuss with learners their reasons for answering in a particular manner. Items should then be revised or discarded accordingly.

Many computer scoring systems provide the instructor with a column labelled *correlation* or point bi-serial correlation rather than the discrimination index. This statistic provides the same general information as the discrimination index and can be interpreted in the same way. It indicates the extent to which each item is related to (correlated with) the total test score. The similarity may not be immediately obvious: if the responses on an individual item are related to the responses on the total test, this indicates that the individuals who responded correctly to the item also likely did well on the test. An instructor who is calculating item statistics by hand would probably prefer to use the discrimination index; however the formula for the point bi-serial correlation may be of assistance to some individuals in the interpretation of computer-produced analyses.

$$Point\ bi\text{–}serial\ correlation\ (r) = \frac{\overline{X_U} - \overline{X_L}}{s} \cdot \sqrt{pc\ pi}$$

where $\overline{X_U}$ = the mean (average) score of students in the upper group (the top *one-half* of the group), $\overline{X_L}$ = the mean score of students in the lower group (the lower one-half), s = the standard deviation of the total group, pc = the percentage of the students who answered the item correctly, pi = the percentage of the students who answered the item incorrectly.

The point bi-serial correlation can range from −1 to +1, as can the discrimination index, and the interpretation of the results is the same. For the norm-referenced test, it is expected that the correlations are high, or at least above 0.3, and for the criterion-referenced test, they should be positive, though not necessarily greater than zero. The item flaws which commonly produce unexpected point bi-serial correlations are identical to those listed for the discrimination index.

The *reliability* and validity of an instructor-made objectively scored test can be checked to some extent. The review process provides an assessment of content validity, and the item analysis yields information as to internal consistency (reliability). Further analyses are often not practical, but whenever the required information is available, it may be useful to calculate some additional statistics. For example, if the same test is given to the same students on two different occasions, the test-retest reliability (stability) can be estimated by determining the correlation between the two sets of test results. Although different formulae are available, if a correlation is being calculated by hand or with a calculator, the following procedure is the easiest:

$$r = \frac{N \, \Sigma XY - (\Sigma X)(\Sigma Y)}{\sqrt{[N \, \Sigma X^2 - (\Sigma X)^2] \, [N \, \Sigma Y^2 - (\Sigma Y)^2]}}$$

where N = the number of learners; ΣXY = the sum of the products of learners' scores on the two tests (i.e., for each learner, multiply the first test score (X) by the second test score (Y) and add these products); ΣX = the sum of the first test scores; ΣY = the sum of the second test scores; ΣX^2 = the sum of the first test scores after each has been squared; $(\Sigma X)^2$ = the sum of the first test scores, which is then squared; ΣY^2 = the sum of the second test scores after each has been squared, $(\Sigma Y)^2$ = the sum of the second test scores, which is then squared.

For a test to have good test-retest reliability, the correlation should be +0.6 or higher.

Estimates of concurrent or predictive validity of the objectively scored test can be obtained when other measures of the same content or set of objectives for the same learners are available. Correlations are calculated using the same formula as given for stability; however, it is not necessarily expected that the correlation would be as high as for test-retest reliability. If, for example, the two test formats are different, the effect of this will yield a less strong relationship between the two measures.

Essays, oral tests, and observation techniques. The first step in the test review and revision process is a review by colleagues or subject area experts. Anyone who is asked to review the instrument should be provided with the objectives being measured and be asked to judge the degree to which they are being accurately assessed. In addition, it is particularly valuable to ask a reviewer to check for any ambiguous wording of items or any cases where items are open to more than one interpretation. If time permits, it may also be useful in the case of the essay or oral test, to ask the reviewer to produce a model answer and to check for discrepancies with expected learner responses.

Clearly the relevant form of reliability for the subjectively scored test will be *inter-rater reliability*. Although it may not be practical in some situations, it is useful to check this aspect whenever possible; for summative evaluation (decision-making), this is especially important. Inter-rater reliability is estimated by having two or more individuals assess the same learners' products or performances and then calculating the correlation between the sets of scores. Many statistical techniques are available; however for the instructor, the most straightforward procedure is to use the correlation formula given on page 175. In order to conclude that inter-rater reliability does exist, the resulting correlation should be +.6 or higher, although this will vary with the particular type of learning being evaluated. The assessment of affective learning may produce a lower inter-rater reliability coefficient using observation techniques due to the interpretation required.

When the practical situation permits, the most useful form of validity to assess is *concurrent validity*. If any other measure of the same learning has been obtained, a correlation can be calculated between the two tests using the formula given previously. The expected correlation would be +.4 or higher.

Summary. The test review and revision process seems formidable. In many informal adult education settings, where grades are not assigned and decisions are not based on evaluation results, the process (except, perhaps, collegial review) is probably not necessary. Even in many more formal courses, it seems that the time required to analyze the quality of a test is not practical. However, many college and university instructors routinely perform item analysis and often ask a peer for comments on an evaluation technique—this is test review and revision. In addition, adult educators often, at one time or another, become involved in the development of curriculum packages, of modules, of individualized instruction, of certification examinations, etc. In these cases, test review and revision is essential.

When an evaluation technique is developed, the *assumption* is made that it measures what it is supposed to measure. When we get strange results, we tend to blame the learner. But regardless of the care that is taken in test development, there can be aspects of the technique itself which distort the results of the evaluation. Test review will help to determine what mistakes have been made in test construction.

Grading

Adult educators working in formal learning settings will often be required to submit a grade for their learners, a procedure which seems to contradict adult education principles. (Especially when the institution doesn't like "all A's" or "all B's" on the grade sheet!) Most instructors agree that grading is the least pleasant aspect of teaching.

Looking for a moment at the positive side, grades do communicate to other instructors, administrators, and potential employers the level of achievement of the learner. Grades also provide information to and act as a motivator or reinforcer for some learners (though many adults are frightened or threatened by grades). In many settings, they are simply necessary as a part of a selection process: accepting individuals into graduate school or medical school, deciding who meets the standards of a program, ranking learners for awards or other types of recognition. This, of course, is norm-referenced evaluation, which many adult educators do not accept as appropriate for their learners.

Planning a Grading System

When grading must be done, it should be done systematically and fairly. The first step is the selection of an appropriate model or approach. The selection should be based on variables such as the level of instruction, subject area, whether the instruction is required or not, instructor preference, and student characteristics.

In the norm-referenced model, grades are assigned on the basis of the learner's relative standing in a group. This approach can simply involve the ranking of individuals on evaluation results, or it can include the use of a predetermined distribution of grades (such as the normal curve). This model is really only appropriate when learners will be selected for further study, for certification, etc. The use of the normal curve as a grading distribution has special problems: it is not usually the case that one group of learners actually do possess a normal distribution of ability or achievement. The normal distribution is based on large random samples of a population, and instructional groups are often small or self-selected. Use with caution! Or with standardized tests and large groups.

In the criterion-referenced model, grades are assigned on the basis of mastery of a set of objectives. Criterion-referenced evaluation may lead to a pass/fail grading system, or may be modified to include a small number of categories in order to meet institutional requirements. Cut-off points (criteria) for the grades are planned in advance, and regardless of the distribution of results, learners receive a grade which reflects their mastery of the objectives

Contract grading is a form of the criterion-referenced approach which is particularly appropriate for the adult learner. Instructor and learner negotiate and agree to a certain quality and quantity of work for a specific grade. For example, it may be agreed that if the learner attends all sessions and participates in all activities, a C grade will be given; if, in addition, the individual chooses to write two essays on a relevant topic, a B grade will be given; and so on. With this approach, the adult learner has input into the evaluation system and is reassured about the grade he or she will receive.

Contract grades can be based on the growth or improvement that the learner demonstrates in an area. In many situations, it is more important that the learner improves than that he or she attains a particular level of achievement. Contracts can be negotiated on this basis.

Many adult educators recommend self-evaluation or peer evaluation as a basis for grading. This approach fits in nicely with the use of contracts and has the added advantage of facilitating self-evaluation skills for the learner. It is important though, that the instructor have input into the process at some level; the learner is not a subject expert and may have difficulty in judging the quality or degree of improvement of the work undertaken.

The second step in planning a grading system is the design of a weighting system for all relevant evaluation components. Many instructors will assign weights arbitrarily, juggling the numbers so that they add up to 100%. A weighting system should be based on characteristics of the instructional situation. The amount of time spent on the objectives being evaluated should be represented in some way, and the importance of the learning should be considered. For example, in professional training, there is often a set of essential skills (e.g. safety checks in administering medication) which must contribute extensively to a final grade. At times, if an essential skill is not mastered, the learner must not pass, regardless of the performance on other objectives. Similarly, when mastery of some objectives is a prerequisite for further study or is necessary for the writing of a certification examination, the instructor may wish to weight that learning more highly in the grading scheme. In some cases, the instructor may wish also to consider the level of learning being assessed. The higher levels of learning may be given more weight than the lower levels of learning in a final grade.

It can be useful to devise a matrix of objectives by evaluation techniques, indicating the time spent on each objective by the learners and the importance of that objective in terms of the training, program, future learning, etc. Such a procedure will ensure that evaluation of each objective is considered in the grading plan, and that the time and importance variables are used to select weights.

The third step in planning the grading procedure is to select a method for combining the various evaluation results that will yield the composite grade. It is too often the case that the instructor merely calculates the sum of scores throughout the instruction and assigns grades on that basis. When two sets of scores have different variances (the degree to which the results are spread out), which they almost always do, the adding of the raw numbers results in a distortion of the sum. A score of 60 on a test where the scores range from 50 to 65 does not carry the same meaning as a score of 60 on a test where the scores range from 35 to 60. When they are added together, the underlying assumption is that they mean the same thing. In addition, when scores on two tests are highly related to each other, the addition of the raw scores will compound any error that may exist in the measurement. It is important, therefore, to conduct a simple statistical manipulation of the scores before obtaining a composite score or grade. All results are converted to standard scores by calculating:

$$z = 10 \left(\frac{X - \overline{X}}{s} \right) + 50$$

where z = the standard score, X = the individual learner scores, $\overline{X}$ = the average of all individual scores, s = the standard deviation of all scores.

Standard scores may be added to yield composite scores which can then be converted into grades.

CHAPTER SEVEN

EVALUATING THE INSTRUCTION

In any instructional situation, informal evaluation of instruction occurs. The instructor lecturing to a large class will observe student unrest, lack of response, or a drop in attendance and will attempt to modify the teaching strategies. The workshop leader who notes lack of participation in exercises or minimal contribution to discussions will quickly realize that some change needs to be made to yield effective instruction. And of course if it becomes clear that the learner is not understanding the content of the session, the ultimate criterion of effective teaching is not being met, and a new strategy will be tried.

This informal and on-going evaluation of instruction does yield useful information; however it does not provide a comprehensive picture of the teaching or the course, and it rarely gives the instructor the kind of feedback that can be directly used to make improvements. It is essential that a systematic evaluation of the instruction be planned.

For our purposes in this chapter, evaluation of instruction will be defined as the systematic collection of information regarding the quality of the instruction for either the purpose of making improvements or making decisions. The evaluation of instruction has long been a controversial issue, in part because it is commonly associated solely with the use of student questionnaires, a technique which does have limitations. Some of the basic concerns which arise when evaluation is being discussed will be presented in this first section. In the remainder of the chapter, a procedure for designing and conducting an instructional evaluation will be outlined.

The first basic issue which is often raised is whether or not teaching can be evaluated at all. Many educators feel that teaching is an art, or, at best, a skill which varies considerably from individual to individual, making it difficult to quantify in any way. This is an understandable concern and probably reflects, at least in part, a general reluctance to have our performance judged. It is true that instructors have different styles, some of which are more effective for different students, and it is also true that the quality of any performance is difficult to judge (as was seen in the chapter on evaluation of learner performance). However, many aspects of good teaching have been isolated by educational researchers (e.g. the necessity for regular feedback, the importance of active learner participation, the value of clear expectations), and these specific behaviors can be judged by participants in the learning process, by other instructors, and by the instructor involved. We can determine, with some degree of accuracy, whether or not learners enjoy the instruction, whether they are learning, and whether other subject area experts see the content as being adequately dealt with.

A second concern that is often raised is the degree to which students can accurately judge the quality of the instruction. They are students, after all, and they probably do not realize the value of the course until long after they leave; in the interim they probably judge the instruction on the basis of the popularity of the instructor. (Is he a nice guy?) Again, this is an understandable concern; students are generally unable to judge, for example, the knowledge of the instructor in the subject area. First, the audience, although a valuable part of any evaluation, should not be the sole contributor of information; colleagues are more prepared to assess the comprehensiveness of an instructional plan than are learners. Second, the audience *is* able to reliably judge the instructor's performance, and this judgement will generally be consistent with judgements provided long after the instruction has taken place (cf. Marsh, 1977). Third, the issue of the "popularity contest" has been investigated in detail by educational researchers (cf. Williams & Ware, 1977), the general conclusion being that learners are able to discriminate between the dynamic popular instructor who does not present substantial content and the instructor who provides challenging and relevant information.

Another common concern among instructors is that systematic evaluation of their teaching will result in comparisons to other instructors which cannot be valid. Probably the greatest fear is that instructors will be ranked and administrative or personnel decisions made on that basis, when, in fact, the instructional situations are quite different. This is a valid concern. Several aspects of the instructional situation have been shown to influence evaluations of instruction (class size, level of instruction, subject area, motivation for taking the course), and therefore comparisons based on audience ratings must be made with great caution (cf. Cranton & Smith, 1986). However, for the instructor who is designing instruction and including an evaluation component in the design, this issue should not arise. The primary purpose of the evaluation will be the improvement of instruction; as such it will be designed specifically for the instructional situation and will not be useful for comparative analyses. It is strongly recommended that evaluation for administrative decision making be treated separately.

In summary, although the evaluation of instruction may be a threatening process, and although it is a process which must be conducted with care, it also provides essential information regarding the instruction. If we, as instructors, consider ourselves as learners (learning to teach), we also need regular and comprehensive and fair feedback about the instruction in order to improve our performance. Just as care must be taken to ensure useful feedback for participants' learning, care must also be taken to collect appropriate information about the quality of instruction.

Planning the Evaluation Procedure

The process of instructional evaluation will be described in six steps: specifying the purpose of the evaluation; selecting the aspects of the instruction to be evaluated; selecting the sources of information; selecting or developing the techniques for collecting information; developing criteria for the interpretation of the information; and collecting and using the information. This process is an adaptation and summary of the McGill Evaluation System (Cranton, 1982a); however, similar procedures are described by most instructional evaluators.

Purpose of the Evaluation

Evaluations of instruction are usually conducted for one or more of three reasons: to improve the instruction, to make administrative decisions including program and personnel decisions, and to aid participators in selecting courses, workshops, or other types of sessions. For the designer of instruction the first purpose is most likely the primary one. As a part of planning instruction, it is essential to consider the collection of information, which will lead to on-going changes in the teaching strategies and activities *during* instruction and in future offerings in the same area. It is this purpose that will be the focus for the remainder of the chapter. For a discussion of other purposes, the reader should refer to Cranton (1982a), Centra (1979), Fuhrmann and Grasha (1983), or any of the large number of books on evaluation of instruction.

Aspects of Instruction to be Evaluated

The most common mistake made by instructors in planning an evaluation is to begin with an instrument, usually a questionnaire, for collecting information. The questionnaire then determines the nature of the information collected when that decision should be based on the need of the instructor for specific data. In other words, you should know what you want to find out before you start asking questions.

Information can be collected to confirm teaching strengths, to specify suspected weaknesses, or to check out a new strategy or activity or reading. For convenience, aspects of instruction will be separated into aspects of the course (or workshop, seminar, or any other instructional format) and of the teaching performance, though in practice this distinction need not be maintained.

Course components. The instructor who has conscientiously applied the planning principles outlined here will have at this point: a list of objectives, a planned sequence, a selected set of methods and materials, and techniques for the evaluation of participants' learning. Depending on the situation, the instructor may wish to obtain feedback on the effectiveness of some or all of the following components:

- Objectives (clarity, relevance)
- Sequence
- Readings, books
- Audio or visual media
- Outside resources (guest speakers, clinical facilities, library services, etc.)
- Internal resources (labs, computer facilities, physical environment)
- Special methods (modules, computer assisted instruction, field trips)
- Assignments, projects
- Techniques for providing feedback, evaluation
- Grading procedures, where relevant

Instructional components should be selected about which something can be done. There is no point in finding out that everyone hates the room you are working in if no other room is available; in fact, it will undoubtedly be frustrating for your audience if you ask for that feedback and then do not make a change based on it. Also, it is not usually wise to evaluate all aspects at one time; the evaluation will become too long and complex, and most instructors are unable or unwilling to make a large number of changes in any one situation.

Teaching performance. The second aspect of the evaluation to be considered is the actual teaching performance—the instructor's behavior with the learners. Although teaching styles and roles vary considerably from one individual to another and from one instructional situation to another, there are several basic teaching skills that should be visible in any instructional situation. Researchers have attempted to identify the underlying components of effective teaching. The general consensus is that four major factors emerge: presentation skill (the ability to convey information in a clear, interesting, relevant, and stimulating way); rapport with the audience (the ability to establish and maintain empathy with, concern for, and interaction with the group); structure (the tendency to have and follow a definite outline or schedule that facilitates learning); and the provision of feedback or the use of fair evaluation strategies. For the purpose of evaluating teaching skills, these categories can be further subdivided.

- Establishing learner expectations
- Logical organization of content
- Pacing
- Elaboration (clarifying or developing an idea or topic)
- Asking questions
- Responding to questions
- Facilitating learner participation
- Closure (integration of ideas at the end of a session)
- Evaluation and feedback on learning
- Selecting the appropriate level of difficulty/challenge
- Using a variety of methods and materials
- Creativity of methods
- Management of time and activities
- Flexibility and individualization
- Interpersonal relations
- Creating a learning environment
- Stimulating interest and enthusiasm
- Establishing a frame of reference (relating to learners' experiences)
- Identifying and clarifying values

Although the research on instructional effectiveness has not yet considered it, the instructor of adults should also add to this list:

- Encouraging self-directed learning (audience input into the instruction)

Again, it is important not to try to evaluate everything at once and to be sure that the time and resources exist to make improvements to the aspects that are evaluated.

Sources of Information

The third step in planning the evaluation of instruction is to select the appropriate sources of information for the aspects of the situation that will be evaluated. The learners should always be included since they are the "consumers" of the instruction, but they may not have the expertise to provide information on some components of instruction. It is advisable to use more than one source of information in all situations as a cross-check. Information obtained from any one source will be influenced by a number of circumstances. Generally, different sources of information provide different types of information.

- Colleagues

  Judgements about content, materials resources, organization

- Learners

  Ratings of the effectiveness of teaching skills
  Comments on the difficulty level, relevance of content, clarity of objectives
  Amount learned

- Professional Associations

  Relevance of instruction to the profession

- Administrators

  Relevance of instruction to the program

- Self

  Effectiveness of teaching skills
  Amount of learning

- Individuals who previously completed the instruction

  Relevance of instruction to profession, career, trade, etc.

- Government agencies

  Curriculum requirements, professional requirements

- Community agencies

  Relevance of instruction to audience needs, employment trends, type of training required
  Individuals who dropped out or left the instruction
  Effectiveness of teaching skills
  Relevance of content

- Other institutions

  Instruction content and organization

- Support services

  Information on use of library, computer services, drop-in centres, counselling services, etc.

Obviously, the appropriateness of a source of information depends on the instructional situation. A university-level course in the arts will be quite different from professional training, basic academic upgrading, or a general interest session. The adult educator should be creative in looking for sources of information that are relevant to his or her situation; valuable insights on the effectiveness of the instruction can be obtained by asking questions of a variety of individuals or groups.

Techniques for Collecting Information

When we think of evaluation of instruction, we think of questionnaires. The questionnaire *does* provide a quick and reliable way of getting information. It does, however, have its limitations and should never be relied on exclusively. Extensive research has been done on the use of ratings or questionnaires, some of which will be summarized at the end of this chapter.

As we saw with sources of information, different techniques will yield different types of information: much more detail can be obtained from an interview or discussion than from a rating scale; open-ended comments can reveal unexpected reactions; videotapes can provide a means of systematically observing your own behavior. The most commonly used techniques will be described, followed by information on the selection or development of each technique.

Interviews are face-to-face individual question and answer sessions. They may be preplanned and fairly structured or completely open-ended and flexible. They are most appropriate for obtaining information that cannot be easily quantified or for uncovering unexpected feelings and reactions. They generally provide detailed, in-depth information on a small number of topics and address the "why" rather than the "what" questions. Interviews can also be used with small groups of individuals where they tend to be less time-consuming, but are also less likely to be completely representative of the interviewees' viewpoints. Interview data of any kind are time-consuming and difficult to analyze but yield rich results.

Observations involve watching the instruction in progress. Specific behaviors may be observed and recorded. The emphasis is often on the occurrence of the behavior; however, ratings or judgements may be made. Observers should be trained and some systematic procedure should be used for recording the observations. Observations are most useful in obtaining detailed information on specific behaviors or skills of the instructor. They are relatively time-consuming to conduct, but when carefully and systematically done, yield direct and useful data.

Comments may be informal or formal records. Individuals or groups can be asked to record their feelings, reactions, and attitudes to various aspects of the instruction. Comments are particularly useful in obtaining unexpected reactions from the audience. However, they are difficult to analyze and do have the tendency to yield unrepresentative data (very positive or very negative comments will be over-represented).

Questionnaires may include ratings of instruction or open-ended questions. When the audience is large, questionnaires are quick, practical, and a generally reliable way of collecting information about attitudes toward the instruction. They do not allow the respondent as much freedom in commenting as do interviews and therefore may not assess unexpected reactions. Also, a poorly constructed questionnaire can easily yield biased responses.

Measures of *participants' learning* may be used as one indication of instructional effectiveness. However, many variables influence learning, and this technique cannot be used as the sole criterion for improvement.

Content and task analysis are techniques for analyzing instructional materials (objectives, outlines, planning notes). These procedures were described in Chapter Four in relation to the sequencing of instruction but can also be conducted by colleagues or other subject area experts in the review of materials. They are useful for assessing the organization of instructional materials, but they are time-consuming and require some training to conduct.

Videotapes and tape recordings provide a lasting record of observations of instruction. The great advantage here is that the instructor can view his or her own teaching and analyze the effectiveness of specific behaviors. Although it is argued that the presence of the recording equipment will change the performance, this effect does not tend to last beyond the introduction to its use.

The selection of an appropriate technique for collecting information will depend on the characteristics of the instructional situation, the aspects of instruction being evaluated, and the sources of information being used. The use of a questionnaire, for example, with a small number of participants (less than 15 or so) will not tend to yield reliable results; the use of interviews with large numbers of individuals will provide completely unmanageable results when analysis is attempted; videotapes cannot be easily used in practical settings such as shops or hospitals.

When the evaluation is being conducted for improvement purposes, it is usually more relevant to design the measurement technique for the specific situation in which it will be used. Evaluators and researchers have developed and tested many instruments (particularly questionnaires), and a selection of these are listed at the end of the chapter. However, an individual instructor most often finds that no one published instrument is suitable to his or her evaluation. It becomes important, therefore, that instructors are aware of the fundamental guidelines for constructing (or adapting) their own techniques. The avoidance of some simple common errors can greatly increase the accuracy of the information collected.

1. Interviews. Interview formats vary considerably from one situation to another. It is generally advisable to use a structured or a semi-structured format; that is, to plan the questions that will be asked, to include some follow-up questions (probes), and to carefully consider the areas that will be covered during the interview. When a session is conducted with a small group of individuals, it is useful to increase the structure of the format and build in a strategy for attempting to include each respondent's opinions. Some guidelines for developing an interview format include:

- Be specific and direct, leaving no room for subjective interpretation of the questions on the part of the person being interviewed;

- Be clear; avoid jargon or vague phrases;

- Be concise; people are devoting time to the endeavor;

- Be flexible; useful information can be obtained if individuals have an opportunity to express themselves freely at some point during the interview;

- Be objective; do not lead the interviewee to express your own opinions;

- Record interviews (with the permission of the interviewee) or develop a system for recording responses.

2. Observations. Observations should be systematic and structured. The observer must know which behaviors to look for and have an objective and consistent means of recording them. The guidelines for conducting observations of instruction are identical to those for conducting observations of learner performance: a checklist or a rating scale or some combination of the two formats should be used (see Chapter Six, p. 167).

3. Comments. Gathering comments or reviews is relatively easy, but interpreting the results can be a challenging task. If a structured format for the recording of comments (such as described in Chapter Six, p. 168) is utilized, results can be summarized in terms of the frequencies of responses in each category. In order to collect information about unanticipated side-effects, however, a fairly unstructured format should be used. Responses will then require categorization after they are collected. All responses should be read through carefully, then a set of categories developed which seem to describe the nature of the results. Comments will then be reviewed again and categorization attempted; usually the categories require at least one and sometimes two or three revisions before the results are "captured" by the analysis. Bogdan and Taylor (1975) provide further detail on the use and analysis of comments; Sherman and Taylor (1975) discuss the use of comments in evaluation of instruction for improvement.

4. Questionnaires. As mentioned previously, many published questionnaires are available. A summary of twelve comprehensive systems has been compiled by Abrami and Murphy (1981). Bergquist and Phillips' (1975) handbook on faculty development contains examples of instruments. Knowles (1980) presents questionnaires designed for use with adult audiences. Fuhrmann and Grasha (1983) provide some examples for college-level instruction. When a published instrument *is* suitable, or when items from a published instrument are appropriate, they should be used. Some questionnaire systems consist of a selection of items related to specific aspects of instruction; if reliability and validity data are provided, this approach is an ideal one for an individual instructor to take.

When items are developed by the instructor for a unique setting, care should be taken to ensure that the statements or questions are clear, straightforward, and as objective as possible.

- Be clear and unambiguous; items should not be open to interpretation by the respondent;

- Include only one behavior or characteristic in each item;

- Design a response scale which matches the content of the item (e.g. strongly agree, agree, disagree, strongly disagree; excellent, good, poor, unacceptable; almost always, often, sometimes, almost never);

- Select the number of points (between three and seven) to be used on the scale and clearly define each point;

- Ensure that there are an equal number of positive and negative points on the scale;

- Keep the total number of items to a minimum (never more 30).

5. Measures of participants' learning. Guidelines for assessing learning are described in detail in Chapter Six. It should be remembered that many variables, in addition to the quality of the instruction, affect learning, and this cannot be used as a sole indicator of effectiveness.

6. Task and content analysis. Guidelines for examining the structure of the content of instruction through task and content analysis are provided in detail in Chapter Three. These techniques can be applied by the instructor him or herself or by a colleague when one of the aspects being evaluated is the organization or structure of the instruction.

7. Video or tape recordings. The use of video or tape recordings requires the same type of planning as does live observation of instruction. A checklist or rating scale (see above) of the specific aspects being evaluated should be used. Even when the recording is being examined quite informally, the results will be more useful when viewed in a systematic manner.

Setting Criteria for the Evaluation

Before the data are collected for the evaluation, it is important to consider how they will be used to make decisions or plan changes. This step is analogous to formulating research hypotheses: if criteria are set before the information is collected, they will lead to more objective and systematic decisions. Admittedly, setting the criteria for the evaluation of instruction is a complex and somewhat arbitrary task. Many variables affect the teaching and learning process. It is possible, however, to set standards, or a range of standards, keeping in mind that the measurement will not be precise, and revisions to these standards may be required as the evaluation continues.

When the purpose of an evaluation is the improvement of instruction, the consequences of a wrong decision are not serious. It is preferable to set the criteria low; at worst, this will lead to improvements that are not necessary. A general procedure is outlined below.

1. Using the aspects of instruction that were selected for evaluation, along with the items or questions that were developed to measure those aspects, categorize or order them according to their perceived importance. For example, in professional training, field experience may be the most important component of the instruction; in a small discussion-oriented session, instructor skill as a discussion leader may have first priority.

2. Considering the time and resources available, decide the maximum number of areas in which changes could be made at this time. Some changes are obviously more time-consuming than others (e.g. revising the content and organization of the instruction versus selecting a new reading or film). Be practical in deciding how much can be done.

3. For each aspect and for each source of information, predict the responses to the questions being asked.

4. Set criteria using one or more of the following techniques:

a. Specify percentages or frequencies of responses below which that aspect of instruction will be a candidate for change. For example, it could be decided that if more than 30% of the audience are dissatisfied with the sequence of topics, a change will be made. Criteria should be set separately for each aspect of the instruction being evaluated, and all relevant sources of information should be considered.

b. When the setting of specific criteria seems too arbitrary, a range can be used. For example, the criterion for the evaluation of the workload in a college-level course could be that if between 30% and 50% of the questionnaire responses are negative, students will be interviewed to obtain further information.

c. A "tailored evaluation technique" can be used to establish a range of criteria. Evaluation results are considered until the trend toward positive or negative responses becomes clear. Further evaluation continues (possibly with a change to another technique) until the majority of the responses are positive or negative. This strategy is useful with interviews, discussions, comments, and reviews.

d. Specify the number of areas in which improvements will be made, regardless of the absolute level of the responses. For example, it could be decided that the three aspects of instruction receiving the lowest evaluation results would be changed.

e. Discrepancies between expected or predicted ratings and obtained ratings can be used as criteria for change, or as an indication that further evaluation is required.

In summary, the setting of evaluation criteria prior to the collection of information will lead to more objective and systematic interpretation of results. One of the most common failings in the evaluation of instruction is the under-utilization of results: the instructor who routinely hands out a questionnaire near the end of a session, glances through the responses, and cannot determine what changes may be required. The results are put into a file folder, labelled "Evaluation of ...," and that is the end of the process. When criteria are planned in advance, the change process is facilitated.

Collecting and Interpreting Information

For any evaluation that has been carefully planned, the data collection and interpretation is usually straightforward. However, the results can be influenced to some extent by variables such as the directions given during questionnaire administration, the timing of the data collection (e.g. immediately before or after an unusual event), anonymity of responses, and the environment in which the information is collected. Some guidelines for data collection are listed below.

1. Questionnaires, comment forms, etc., should be completed anonymously. In situations where it is useful to follow up on responses or to look at the relationships among several measures, code names or numbers can be used.

2. Clear and accurate directions should be provided for any respondents, whether learners, colleagues, professional groups, administrators. The directions should include a statement as to the purpose of the evaluation and the confidentiality of responses.

3. If it is practical, interviews, discussions, and observations should be conducted by an individual who is not directly affected by the results of the evaluation.

4. Adequate time must be provided for the completion of forms or any other data collection techniques. They should never be handed out at the end of the workshop time with the statement, "oh, would you mind filling this out before you leave." Also, mailed-in responses tend not to be completely representative of participants. Evaluation is an essential part of instruction; it deserves time.

5. Evaluation information should not be collected immediately before or after any unusual event (guest speaker, film, test, holiday, and so on).

6. Information should be collected after participants have had sufficient time to become familiar with the instructor and the content but (for purposes of improvement) while there is still sufficient time to make changes in the instruction.

7. Information should be collected in a relaxed or a natural setting. Do not, for example, have participants come to your office one at a time for an interview, unless that is a procedure which is used in other aspects of the instruction.

8. Whenever possible, cross-check your information with another source to make sure that changes will not be based on inaccurate or biased perceptions.

The analysis of evaluation information varies for each of the techniques described previously. It generally consists of no more than determining frequencies of responses, average responses, and at times, correlations among different measures. Analyses for each of the data collection techniques will be described briefly.

1. The analysis of interview results consists of describing responses in categories. When the interviews are structured or semi-structured, the categories can be determined in advance and modified as necessary. When the interviews are unstructured, categories are created after reading through (or listening to) the responses. The summary of results will then be the frequencies of responses in each category, possibly accompanied by a file of sample answers for each category.

2. Observations are conducted using checklists or rating scales of the behaviors or characteristics being evaluated. The analysis of results consists of determining the frequencies of checks or ratings for each item. Inter-rater reliability can be estimated by calculating the correlation between two observer's responses; however, in individual evaluations for improvement, these data are most often not available.

3. Comments or reviews are analyzed in a manner similar to interviews. That is, responses are categorized and then summarized by determining the frequencies of statements that fall into each category.

4. Questionnaire results can be analyzed using quite sophisticated statistical techniques. However, for the instructor concerned with improvement, the frequencies of responses for each point on the scale and possibly item means or averages are adequate. Items should *never* be added to obtain a total score—different skills are being assessed and a total score is meaningless. In some cases, correlations among items or between specific items and other measures may be useful or interesting. There is a danger, with questionnaire results, to attach too much meaning to the numbers; one is tempted to treat them as exact measures because they can be manipulated statistically. It should be remembered that there is error in the measurement and that results are affected by many variables; an item mean of 3.2 is not different in any meaningful way from an item mean of 3.1. Look for trends and obvious differences in the same way that you would in examining interview results.

5. The analysis of measures of participants' learning depends, of course, on the type of technique being used, as was discussed in Chapter Six. The reporting of results in the evaluation of instruction may take any form preferred by the instructor (percentages, percentiles, letter grades, anecdotal records, sample projects). If measures from different instruments are being combined, it is essential to calculate standard scores or adjusted scores before adding results (see p. 179).

6. Content and task analyses require no statistical treatment. Discrepancies between an instructor analysis and one conducted by a colleague may indicate that a change in the course organization should be made. Situations where the evaluation of participants' learning does not validate the analysis (e.g. a skill can be mastered without its prerequisite) also indicate a problem in the sequencing. If it is necessary to report results, it can be done in terms of the number of discrepancies or errors found.

7. Videotapes and tape recordings are analyzed in the same manner as live observations. It is possible, however, to time-sample the observation; that is, to record every 5, 10, or 15 seconds the behavior which is occurring at that time. This technique generally yields a more representative sample of the instructional process.

The interpretation of evaluation results is done on the basis of the criteria developed before the data collection began. Once the information is analyzed, the criteria are used to determine which areas are in need of change. At times, it becomes apparent at this stage that the predetermined criteria are not realistic. When this is the case, the evaluation results should be set aside and the criteria reconsidered. Every attempt should be made to modify the criteria not solely on the basis of the results, but rather to review the original plans objectively. It is usually helpful to have a colleague assist in this process.

Summary of the Research on the Evaluation of Instruction

The importance of evaluating instruction cannot be over-emphasized. And yet evaluation remains a controversial issue in education. Instructors feel that teaching cannot be accurately or reliably judged, that evaluation does not truly capture the essence of teaching. In order to address these issues further, some of the research on evaluation of instruction will be described.

Defining Effective Instruction

For the last twenty years, researchers have attempted to define effective instruction through the results of evaluation, usually student questionnaire results. These analyses have led, with a fair degree of consistency, to the identification of four major factors underlying teaching behavior: (1) presentation skill—the ability to communicate the content in an interesting, clear, and stimulating manner; (2) rapport—the ability to establish and maintain empathy with, concern for, and interaction with the learner; (3) structure—the tendency to have and follow a clear organization; and (4) evaluation of learning (Kulik & McKeachie, 1975; Cranton, 1982b). Other researchers have asked students, faculty, and alumni groups to describe their perceptions of best and worst teachers using a survey format, or to sort characteristics of instructors into categories (Whitley & Doyle, 1976). Similar results were obtained from this approach. The difficulty with these approaches is that they address the reliability of perceptions of instruction but not necessarily the validity of those perceptions. Ratings or sorting procedures are dependent on the items that are provided to the respondent; these items may be reacted to in a consistent way, but they may not reflect effective instructional behaviors.

Reliability

The reliability of student ratings of instruction has been studied extensively. Questionnaires have been found to be stable over time (Murray, 1980). The internal consistency of rating forms has been supported (Hoffman, 1978), and inter-rater reliability (different groups of learners rating the same instructor) has been found to be high (Marsh, 1982).

Other techniques for collecting evaluation information have not been investigated as to their reliability in assessing instruction. In general, the more subjective the technique, the less reliable it tends to be; for example, interviews are less reliable than questionnaires.

Validity

The validity of student rating forms has been assessed repeatedly. Criterion validity is the extent to which an instrument correlates with another measure of the same variable. A review of the research by Murray (1980) tends to support the criterion validity of the student rating. Correlations between student and colleague ratings tend to be moderate to high; however, some studies report very low correlations. Administrator ratings do not tend to be closely related to student ratings. Alumni ratings do agree with student ratings. Ratings made by trained observers also tend to be correlated with student ratings.

If the questionnaire is a valid measure of teaching effectiveness, it would be expected that the results would be related to the amount of learning taking place. Cohen synthesizes the research on this relationship. Examining the results from 67 courses, the correlations between overall ratings of instruction and student achievement averaged 0.43, a "moderately large effect" (Cohen 1981, 301). Murray reviews ten years of research on the relationship between student ratings of instruction and student learning, describing quite inconsistent results: positive correlations, no correlations, and negative correlations. He concludes that "under most conditions there is a weak to moderate positive correlation" (Murray 1980, 39). Unfortunately, nearly all of this research has been conducted using first-year university courses; its generalizability to other instructional settings has not been demonstrated.

It is also possible that questionnaires measure variables other than instructional effectiveness. It has been shown that ratings are influenced by the size of the class, the level of instruction, whether the course is required or not, the subject area, and combinations of these and other variables (Cranton & Smith, 1986).

The validity of other techniques for collecting information has rarely been addressed in the literature. Murray reviews this area, but does not draw conclusions due to the small amount of research done. He does report that colleague evaluations provide somewhat inconsistent results, apparently determined "in large part by non-instructional factors such as the instructor's knowledge of subject matter or productivity in research" (Murray 1980, 44).

Evaluation and Improvement

Researchers have found it difficult to determine the degree to which evaluation of instruction results in improvement. The complexity of the instructional situation does not lend itself to the use of experimental research techniques, and other approaches cannot yield generalizable results. In a meta-analysis of 30 studies of the effectiveness of student rating feedback, Menges and Brinko (1986) concluded that ratings alone produce a positive but small effect on subsequent ratings, but when ratings were accompanied by other types of feedback or consultation, larger effects were evident. The nature of the instructional situation was not considered in this analysis.

CHAPTER EIGHT

ADULT EDUCATORS: WHO ARE WE?

"The eagerness to construct an empirically verifiable theory of adult learning is inextricably bound up with the quest for professional identity on the part of adult educators... If we could discover certain empirically verifiable differences in learning styles between children (as a generic category) and adults (as a generic category), then we could lay claim to a substantive area for research that would be unchallengeably the property of educators and trainers of adults. Such a claim would provide us with a professional identity. It would ease the sense of insecurity and defensiveness that frequently assails educators and trainers of adults in all settings when faced with the accusation that they are practicing a nondiscipline" (Brookfield 1986, 32–33).

In the thirteen years that I have spent teaching adults how to teach adults, the most commonly asked question from my learners has been some version of, "What's the best way to...?" When I hear my stock answer, "It depends on..." echoed in group discussions or hallway conversations, I reflect that I have probably helped them to understand the *one* general principle of adult education.

I will conclude this practical, structured set of guidelines for the instructor of adults by returning to some of the questions and issues raised in Chapter One. First, the future of adult education and some of the implications of that future for the profession of adult education will be addressed. Second, the issues and conflicts arising from using a systematic model of instructional planning in working with adult learners will be reviewed and discussed. Third, the role of the reflective adult educator in research and theory-building will be addressed.

The Future of Adult Education

In a recent address at Brock University in Ontario, Knowles (1988) pointed out that the median age of the population of North America is dramatically increasing. By the year 2020, in only 30 years, the median age will be about 50 years; in other words, one-half of the population will be over 50 years of age, and one-half of the population will be under 50 years of age. Forty years ago, the median age was 16. Simply, there are and will be many more adult learners than ever before.

Two more pieces of information are needed to complete the picture. We are experiencing unprecedented rapid change in technology and consequently in our culture and way of life. Individuals are forced to or are choosing to change careers at a rate never before observed in history.

It is obvious that adult education will not be lacking "consumers" in the future. Those individuals who are choosing to remain in their present profession or workplace require retraining or updating or professional development to keep up with the changes taking place. Presently, at an average of three times in a lifetime, individuals choose to change their careers; often retraining is an aspect of such a change. And, many individuals, outside of the requirements of their jobs, are actively involved in learning new things and meeting new people in an educational environment.

At present, adult educators comprise a tremendous variety of individuals: those hired specifically for training in business and industry; teachers who are asked to take an adult class in the evenings at their school; people with a special interest or expertise who offer sessions through community or educational agencies; college and university faculty knowledgeable in their discipline but without instructor training; organizers of community or social networks; authors who write self-help books; and individuals who volunteer to help someone else learn. No wonder we lack a professional identity! And yet when the conversation turns to the certification of adult educators, almost everyone draws back in alarm.

The adult educator faces a dilemma: the desire for a professional identity versus the standardization of the profession that would bestow the professional identity. This dilemma is, of course, confounded by the uneasy sensation that we do not really know the best way to teach, facilitate learning, etc., to *be* adult educators.

There are no easy solutions. The growth of adult education as a practice and the development of programs for the training of adult educators at colleges and universities could well lead to a standardization of the role of the adult educator and a certification of the instructor of adults. This, in spite of the fact that we do not have the answers to the "best way" question.

For the practitioner, the only sensible solution is to keep reading, thinking, analyzing, questioning, and criticizing. If the day does arrive when you must apply for your Adult Educator Certificate, you will be prepared.

Issues and Conflicts in the Life of the Adult Educator

"... practical expertise that exists in a moral vacuum can be a dangerous thing" (Brookfield 1986, 285).

The reflective adult educator will daily confront numerous issues and conflicts. Some commonly faced issues will be discussed: working within a prescribed curriculum; writing objectives with the inexperienced learner; working with dependent or other-directed learners; promoting self-evaluation; and dealing with institutional constraints. Some of these issues have been referred to throughout the description of the planning process; others have not yet been addressed.

Prescribed Curriculum

Instructors in a wide variety of disciplines are provided with a prescribed curriculum, including objectives, tests, even learning activities. Most often, this occurs when the program is based on a training model, and when participants are required to write certification examinations or where other standardized requirements exist. Medicine, nursing, dentistry, auto mechanics, hairdressing, electricity, and refrigeration are a sample of the subject areas where this may occur. How can the conscientious adult educator work within these requirements?

I have seen a tremendous variety of responses to this situation in my "how to teach adults" courses and workshops. Some individuals will comment that "none of this is relevant to me; I am given my curriculum" and will subsequently withdraw physically or mentally from the learning process. At the other end of the continuum, I have seen instructors who will put months of effort and energy into developing instructional strategies that will allow their learners to be self-directed, to participate in the teaching and learning process, and to learn how to evaluate their own progress. Others will fight and often change the prescription.

Admittedly, the training of tradesmen or of professionals *does* require standardization. None of us would want to have an electrician work in our homes who had "chosen" to omit the learning of fundamental electrical concepts, or have our hair curled by someone who preferred straight hair and therefore did not choose to learn the techniques required for producing curls.

This issue can be "morally" resolved by understanding and accepting that the learner who has entered a program in electricity or hairdressing has agreed to participate in the training required to become an electrician or a hairdresser. The learner, obviously, cannot design the objectives since he or she is not aware of the components of the training. The learner, in a sense, enters *a contract* with the instructor: I want to be an electrician, and

I accept the training required to make me a competent electrician. Those individuals who realize that the subject area does not match their interests or their abilities make the choice to leave the training. This decision is often mutually negotiated between instructor and learner. Perhaps the principles of adult education are stretched in this scenario, but other components of the prescribed curriculum will be easier to fit.

Most prescribed curricula leave plenty of room for learner- and instructor-designed instructional strategies. There may well be suggested activities or, in the case of prescribed modularized curricula, selected readings and learning tasks. However, the self-directed instructor and the responsible adult learner can easily redesign any suggested or prescribed learning activities. Very rarely is the Great Curriculum Designer watching over the instructional situation. If the objectives are met and the tests are passed, no one really cares how that is accomplished. Options can be provided for individuals; learners can design their own activities to meet the objectives; people can work in groups on a variety of tasks, either learner- or instructor-designed, to meet the objectives; community or field resources can be brought into the learning environment; and, the instructor can negotiate a variety of contracts with individuals in the program.

I once had an electricity instructor in a group of 20 instructors in an Instructor Training Program; he worked with a comprehensive modularized training program where his role had been defined as "manager." He worked five hours a day, five days a week, for three weeks in our program on implementing the principles of adult learning *within* his modularized system. At the end of July, he left, wishing that it was September so that he could see his plan in action. He had entered the program thinking that there was nothing he could do, since he had a prescribed curriculum. I am sure that his learners are still working in groups, designing their own learning activities, and assessing their own progress.

Writing Objectives

The adult education literature tells us that learners should be responsible for setting their own objectives, that they have immediate problems to solve, that they know what they want to learn, and so on. And yet, in practice, in many instructional situations, the learner is not experienced enough with the subject area, or experienced enough with independent learning to be able to set or even contribute to the learning objectives. Imagine the secretary whose office is being computerized and is sent to a beginners' course on word processing. She is anxious, she has not been a student for 15 years, she is afraid that she will be seen as stupid or a slow learner, she has never liked or worked with machines. The instructor begins by asking what the group would like to learn, or asking the group to work together to set their own objectives for the course. Obviously, disaster would result. Most of the learners have been sent to the course and are anxious and have no idea of what skills they should be obtaining.

Brundage and Mackeracher (1980) point out that the adult learner in a new unfamiliar setting will revert to dependent, child-like behaviors and emotions. This is not the time to ask the learner to write his or her own objectives! The sensitive adult educator will provide the structure and direction for the inexperienced learner and will *gradually* seek input from the learner ("I'm not sure if we should do this exercise individually or in groups; what do you think?") until the individuals feel confident enough to make the decisions about their own learning.

Even when the learners have experience with the subject area, they may not have experience with independent learning. They will automatically, based on their previous learning experiences, look to the instructor as the formal authority, the expert. They will say, "You're the instructor, you know best"; they will ask, "What do *you* want us to do?" In every possible way, they will say, "TEACH US." They may be hostile, saying, "I paid for this course and you are the expert and I want you to tell me." Graduate students in adult education will behave in this manner. Unless individuals have been given responsibility for their own learning, they will expect an instructional situation to be similar to what they have experienced in the past; all too often what they have experienced in the past has been instructor-directed.

Once again, the change must be *gradually* introduced. The learners should be provided with objectives and asked for comment and input. Later in the course or session, the instructor can stop and say, "We have done so-and-so, where would you like to go from here?" Those instructors who are working with the same group over time can usually completely turn over the responsibility for setting the objectives to the learners. In a one-day workshop, this will not be possible, but changes can often be made mid-way, based on learner input or questions or concerns. The next time these people attend a one-day workshop they may well ask for more responsibility.

Self-direction

Knowles (1980) and almost every other adult educator emphasizes that adult learners are self-directed. This assumption has been questioned (Brookfield, 1986), but the concept has nevertheless become a slogan of adult education. The practitioner knows that adult learners are often *not* self-directed. To do justice to Knowles, what he says is that adults have a deep psychological need to be self-directing, although they may be dependent in particular temporary situations. He also acknowledges that individuals move from dependence to self-direction at varying rates, and that it is the role of the teacher to nurture this movement. It is the common over-simplification of Knowles' and others' work that has led to the sometimes inappropriate use of learner-directed activities.

Adult learners will be dependent learners when: (1) they are in new, unfamiliar situations where they have no experience with the subject area; (2) they have low self-esteem, related to their personal lives or to the instructional situation; or (3) they have never experienced self-directed learning. The way in which the instructor resolves this issue depends on the characteristics of the learner. The inexperienced learner can gradually be given responsibility for decisions about learning *activities*, then when more familiar with the content and the situation, can be given responsibility for setting objectives and evaluating his or her own progress. Obviously time is required for this approach to be successful; in a one-day workshop, choice of learning activities may be the most self-direction that can be achieved. The learner with low self-esteem will require considerable support, positive feedback, and respect before he or she can comfortably take responsibility for learning. Not much can be achieved in a one-session instructional situation. It is essential, though, to make the effort, perhaps to provide the beginning of a new perception of learning for the individual. The last group, those individuals who simply have never had the opportunity to participate in self-directed learning, are clearly the easiest to work with in this area. Most often, simply providing the opportunity will result immediately in an enthusiastic, talkative audience. They may question the instructor's role, or see the session as "not really learning" (since it was enjoyable), but they will inevitably react positively and seek out other similar learning experiences.

It is sometimes difficult to determine which category or categories a specific audience falls into. However, simple questions about background, previous experience with the topic, reasons for being there, and special interests, along with careful observation of non-verbal behavior, will usually indicate how ready a group is for self-directed learning activities.

Evaluation

The issue of evaluation of learner performance can be a torturous one for the adult educator. The literature advocates learner self-evaluation or self-diagnosis of learning needs. The institution often requires grading and sometimes norm-referenced grading. Any instructor working within a training model must also deal with standards for certification.

As discussed in relation to prescribed curriculum, the instructor of adults can often work effectively within the requirements of a program or institution; in some cases (e.g. the use of norm-referenced grading) the instructor can work to modify the system.

Let's examine the common dilemma of being required to assign grades. This institutional expectation is faced by every college and university instructor and is not easily changeable. Depending on the level of instruction, the characteristics of the audience, and the subject area, a variety of strategies can be used:

1. All individuals can be assigned the same grade at the beginning of the course, conditional upon their meeting clearly described minimum requirements; this strategy removes anxiety about and competition for grades;

2. Individuals can negotiate a contract for the grade they wish to receive with the instructor; again, anxiety and competition are removed, plus flexibility and individualization are introduced into the evaluation process;

3. Learners can select or design activities which they wish to be evaluated on, including the weight they wish each activity to have in the calculation of a final grade; some general guidelines may be preset by the instructor; the audience must be fairly independent for this to be successful; or

4. In addition to selecting their own evaluation activities, learners may also decide whom they wish to judge each product or performance (peers, self, instructor, outside resource people).

Working within a system which requires grades, learners can have complete responsibility for the evaluation of their own progress. Even when objectives are determined by others, learners can assume responsibility for assessing their performance.

Institutional Constraints

"It is obviously absurd to presume that adults learn only during two-hour blocks of time that occur on the same evening, between the same times, each week, and yet the organization of many adult education programs into weekly, two-hour blocks of instruction suggests the implicit acceptance of this bizarre assumption" (Brookfield 1986, 234).

We've all experienced the two- or three-hour block that was not long enough, or far too long. The classroom with the chairs bolted to the floor. The silent building at night with the closed coffee shop. And the locked photocopying room or library. The adult educator rarely has control over the time-table, the physical facilities, or the resources available during instruction. We hardly ever have our own teaching room where we can soften the atmosphere or leave things up on the walls. We come in at night and try not to disturb someone else's room.

The workshop leader or professional development person who does have control will choose a room with comfortable chairs and tables that can be arranged in a circle. He or she will arrange to have coffee delivered, pencils provided, handouts copied, and flip charts available. These small things will create an environment in which everyone feels comfortable and consequently an environment in which everyone enjoys learning.

But what to do in the dark and silent building at night? Once, in facilitating a session on creating an environment which encourages learning at night at a university, I simply said to the group at the beginning of the three-hour block, "Do whatever you can think of doing to this room to make it more inviting for you." The group responded first with bewildered silence and inaction. No one had ever thought of *changing* the room. I, too, remained silent and immobile. Finally, someone said, "I'd like to move that string hanging down from the projector screen, I always look at it and I hate it." I said, "Go move it." Within an hour, we had moved all the furniture in the room, dimmed the lights, moved away all the equipment we were not using, cleaned the blackboards from previous sessions, put up some learner-designed posters (flip chart paper), and brought in coffee and muffins. The group had created an environment that they felt was more conducive to their learning. All subsequent sessions began by re-creating that environment. And I learned a great deal about dealing with institutional constraints.

Relatively small changes can create an environment which can encourage learning and overcome many institutional constraints. Even though the three-hour block may be fixed, breaks can be taken at varying times, depending on the nature of the activities in the session. There is nothing inherently wrong with finishing early or late (as long as all individuals have independent transportation). Coffee and snacks can be brought in by members of the group. Sometimes a key can be obtained to the photocopier. Chairs and tables can almost always be arranged in a circle (if they are nailed to the floor, *do* insist on a room change). The chalkboard can always be erased or covered with flip-chart posters. When a group is comfortable and familiar with one another, sessions can even be moved to the homes of individuals in the group. Sometimes a vacant lounge can be found in the building and used for group work.

At the same time, every adult educator should continue to ask for physical facilities that are conducive to adult learning. Many times institutional scheduling personnel or administrators are not even aware of the needs of the adult learner; repeated requests with a solid rationale can gradually result in a change in institutional constraints.

Theory-Building and Research

The theoretical foundations of adult education were briefly over-viewed in Chapter One. The theoretical bases of our work have been drawn from a wide variety of sources, many of which were not intended to describe the unique characteristics of adult learning. No *one* theory of adult learning or instruction exists and may not even be a reasonable or desirable goal. Research in the area is in its very beginning stages. The majority of the work to date has consisted of survey-type research, de-scribing the characteristics of adults who return to instructional settings or the obstacles that stand in the way of adult learning. A limited amount of research has addressed the validity of the theoretical assumptions underlying practice. We do not know, for example, that adults learn more or more efficiently when they are self-directed; we do not even know that learning is improved when immediate or relevant learning goals are ad-dressed. It is dangerous to generalize from research conducted with chil-dren, and the research on adult learning is scattered and unsystematic.

And yet tens of thousands of adult educators work with millions of adult learners every day in North America. They cannot wait for the answers from the researchers; they have a group to lead, a workshop to facilitate, a class to teach, a graduate student to advise.

What is the role of the adult educator in the world of theory and research? Unfortunately, the gap between the two worlds often seems unbridgeable. Researchers write in journals, using a language that is in-comprehensible to practitioners and rarely communicate directly with the practitioner (unless he or she is a subject in a research study). And practitioners do not have the time, the expertise, or the interest in pursu-ing the scholarly journals. How can we ever hope to do anything useful for either group?

Recently, terms like the "reflective practitioner" and "action research" have come into being, as a result of viewing the person doing the job as the best person to describe that job. The reflective practitioner thinks about, analyzes, criticizes, and talks about what he or she does, perhaps even writes about it. The university researcher engages the practitioner in the design and conduct of "action research." And the two worlds meet, to the benefit of both.

Adult education is a peculiar discipline. Perhaps it is not even a disci-pline. It involves no professional training, it includes a tremendously wide variety of activities, and it has theoretical foundations drawn from diverse areas. If we are *ever* to understand what we do and why we do it and be able to predict the consequences of what we do, it is essential that the practitioner be an integral part of that process.

I would argue that it is essential that the instructor of adults be reflective, critical, analytical, and judgemental and be able to communicate those thoughts to others. No one knows more about the characteristics of the adult learner than the adult instructor who works daily and intensively with a group of adult learners. The future of the practitioner is clear—the need for adult education will only grow. The future of theory-building and research endeavors depends on the practitioner.

REFERENCES

Abrami, P., and V. Murphy
1981   *Catalogue of Twelve Systems for Evaluating Teaching.* Montreal: McGill's Centre for University Teaching and Learning.

Alpert, R., and R.N. Haber
1964   Anxiety in academic achievement situations. *Journal of Abnormal and Social Psychology, 61,* 207–215.

Bergquist, W.H., and S.R. Phillips
1975   *A Handbook for Faculty Development.* Vol. 1. Washington, D.C.: Council for the Advancement of Small Colleges.

Bloom, B.
1956   *Taxonomy of Educational Objectives, Handbook I: Cognitive Domain.* New York: McKay.

Bogdan, R., and S. Taylor
1975   *Introduction to Qualitative Research Methods.* New York: John Wiley & Sons.

Brookfield, S.
1986   *Understanding and Facilitating Adult Learning.* San Francisco: Jossey-Bass.

Brundage, D., and D. Mackeracher
1980   *Adult Learning Principles and their Application to Program Planning.* Toronto: Ontario Institute for Studies in Education.

Bruner, J.
1968   *Towards a Theory of Instruction.* New York: W.W. Norton and Co.

Centra, J.A.
1979   *Determining Faculty Effectiveness.* San Francisco: Jossey-Bass.

Clark, R. (Ed.)
1975   Aptitude-treatment interaction research (Special Issue). *AV Communication Review, 23* (2).

Cohen, P.
1981   Student ratings of instruction and student achievement: A meta-analysis of multisection validity studies. *Review of Educational Research, 51,* 281–309.

Cranton, P.A.

1982a   *McGill Evaluation System: Users' Guide.* Montreal: McGill's Centre for University Teaching and Learning.

1982b   Statistical analyses of evaluation results. Paper presented at the Annual Meeting of the American Educational Research Association, New York.

Cranton, P.A., and R. Smith

1986   A new look at the effect of course characteristics on student ratings of instruction. *American Educational Research Journal, 23,* 117–128.

Cronbach, L.J.

1957   The two disciplines of scientific psychology. *American Psychologist, 12,* 671–684.

Cronbach, L.J., and R.E. Snow

1977   *Aptitudes and Instructional Methods.* New York: Irvington Publishers.

Cross, P.

1981   *Adults as Learners.* San Francisco: Jossey-Bass.

Dale, E.

1969   *Audio-Visual Methods in Teaching* (3rd ed.). New York: Holt, Rinehart and Winston.

Darkenwald, G., and S. Merriam

1983   *Adult Education: Foundations of Practice.* New York: Harper & Row.

Dewey, J.

1916   *Education and Democracy.* New York: Macmillan.

1938   *Experience and Education.* London: Collier Macmillian.

Domino, G.

1975   Let the punishment fit the crime: teacher student interation. *Journal of Educational Research, 65,* 8–11.

Dunn, R., and K. Dunn

1977   How to diagnose learning styles. *Instructor, 87,* 123–144.

Fleishman, E.A.

1964   *The Structure and Measurement of Physical Fitness.* Englewood Cliffs, N.J.: Prentice Hall.

Fleming, M., and W.H. Levie

1978   *Instructional Message Design: Principles from the Behavioral Sciences.* Englewood Cliffs, N.J.: Educational Technology Publications.

Freire, P.

1973   *Education for Critical Consciousness.* London: Sheed and Ward.

Fuhrmann, B., and A. Grasha

1983   *A Practical Handbook for College Teachers.* Boston: Little, Brown and Company.

Gagné, R.M.

1975   *Essentials of Learning for Instruction.* Hinsdale, Illinois: Dryden Press.

1977   *The Conditions of Learning* (3rd ed.). New York: Holt, Rinehart and Winston.

Green, J.A.

1975   *Teacher-made Tests* (2nd ed.). New York: Harper & Row.

Hoffman, R.G.

1978   Variables affecting university student ratings of instructor behavior. *American Educational Research Journal, 15,* 287–289.

Kibler, R.J., L.L. Barker, and D.T. Miles

1970   *Behavioral Objectives and Instruction.* Boston: Allyn and Bacon.

Kiely, Y.

1981   An Investigation of Effective Clinical Teaching. Master's Thesis, Department of Educational Psychology, McGill University.

Knowles, M.S.

1978   *The Adult Learner: A Neglected Species* (2nd ed.). Houston: Gulf.

1980   *The Modern Practice of Adult Education.* New York: Association Press.

1984   *Andragogy in Action: Applying Modern Principles of Adult Learning.* San Francisco: Jossey-Bass.

Krathwohl, D.R., B.S. Bloom, and B.B. Masia

1964   *Taxonomy of Educational Objectives, Handbook II: Affective Domain.* New York: McKay.

Kulik, J.A., and W.J. McKeachie

1975   The evaluation of teachers in higher education. In F.N. Kerlinger (Ed.), *Review of Research in Education.* Vol. 3. Itaska, Illinois: Peacock.

Lindeman, E.

1926   *The Meaning of Adult Education.* Montreal: Harvester House.

Mager, R.F.

1962   *Preparing Instructional Objectives.* Belmont, California: Fearon Publishers.

Marsh, H.W.

1977   The validity of students' evaluations: classroom evaluations of instructors independently nominated as best and worst teachers by graduating seniors. *American Educational Research Journal, 14,* 441–447.

1982 Factors affecting students' evaluations of the same course taught by the same instructor on different occassions. *American Educational Research Journal, 19,* 485–497.

McKeachie, W.J.

1978 *Teaching Tips: A Guidebook for the Beginning College Teacher.* Lexington, Mass.: D.C. Heath & Co.

Mezirow, J.

1977 Perspective transformation. *Studies in Adult Education, 9,* 100–110.

1981 A critical theory of adult learning and education. *Adult Education., 32,* No. 1.

Murray, H.

1980 *Evaluating University Teaching: A Review of Research.* Toronto: Ontario Confederation of University Faculty Associations.

Piaget, J.

1929 *The Child's Conception of the World.* London: Routledge and Kegan Paul.

Rogers, C.R.

1969 *Freedom to Learn.* Columbus, Ohio: Merrill Publishing.

Rotter, J.B.

1966 Generalized expectancies for internal vs external control of reinforcement. *Psychological Monographs, 80,* Whole No. 609.

Salomon, G.

1974 Internalization of filmic operations in relation to individual differences. *Journal of Educational Psychology, 66,* 499–511.

Sax, G.

1968 *Empirical Foundations of Educational Research.* Englewood Cliffs, N.J.: Prentice-Hall.

Sherman, T.M., and S. Taylor

1975 A formative approach to student evaluation of instruction. *Educational Technology,* January, 34–39.

Simpson, E.J.

1966 The Classification of Educational Objectives: Psychomotor Domain. University of Illinois Research Project No. OE 5, 85–104.

Torkelson, G.M.

1975 Conceptualization and Dale's Cone of Experience. Unpublished manuscript, University of Washington, College of Education.

Whitely, S.E., and K.O. Doyle

1976 Implicit theories in student ratings. *American Educational Research Journal, 13,* 241–253.

Williams, R.G., and J.E. Ware
1977   An extended visit with Dr. Fox: Validity of student satisfaction with instructor ratings after repeated exposures to a lecturer. *American Educational Research Journal, 14,* 449–457.

INDEX